UP THE RIVER
ON A LEAKY JUNK
And Other Life Tales

UP THE RIVER ON A LEAKY JUNK
And Other Life Tales

Dava Louise Colcord

New Harbor Press

Up the River on a Leaky Junk, and Other Life Tales

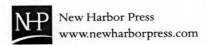 New Harbor Press
www.newharborpress.com

ISBN 978-1-63357-112-9

DEDICATION

This book is dedicated as a memorial to
David, my husband, who taught me about God's love.
David went to be with the Lord on March 28, 2014.
Some day we will be together again praising the Lord for all
eternity.

Dave Beaumont

CONTENTS

FOREWORD

I want to live a spirit-led life, not a logic-led life.

—David Colcord, 1990

Over twenty-five years ago, sitting in an office in a building that no longer exists, in the heart of Atlanta, Georgia, I met Dava and David Colcord. I was a young pastor, fresh out of seminary, working at a megachurch, and had been given the responsibility of overseeing one hundred missionary families and the church's global outreach efforts. On this day, I was invited into the Colcord's world and became privileged to witness what faith with works looks like in the modern church.

Dava began talking, with her laugh interspersed between the words, about what she hoped, knew, and believed that God was going to do with her and David. I listened. For the next six years, I listened and watched as God moved the Colcords in and out of the country for global service. He used them to impact hundreds of international students from universities in the Atlanta area. I saw how God used pain and joy as tools to guide His children. I witnessed how our Heavenly Father transforms obedient faith into real life God glorifying work for His kingdom.

Each time God called Dava and David to something new, it required faith and more sacrifices. I learned to stop questioning what God may be up to in them. I began watching with anticipation for what He was going to do and did. For me, each adventure revealed more and more of who God is. Through the Colcords, my faith and trust in Him were strengthened. When God started calling me to an obedient faith, I said yes to God with confidence. God used the Colcords' life to transform me. I longed for them to stop in my office to report and debrief after each assignment. The next thing I knew, they were coming to share where God was leading next!

In the first meeting we ever had, David said that he wanted to "live a spirit-led life, not a logic-led life." Since David and I were both engineering graduates of Georgia Tech, that statement made a big impression on me. The Colcords have done just this! I encourage you to read about their adventures in Toronto, Macau, China and Hong Kong as well as here in Atlanta.

Observe how the Colcords yielded to the illogical guidance of God in order to gain the eternal rewards of a spirit-led life. You will be glad you did.

Yielding to a Spirit-led Life,

Larry Ragan
Founder CULTURELink Inc.
culturelinkinc.org

October 2016

CULTURELink's mission is to make disciples of those who will make disciples of all nations. Through education, equipping, and exposure, CULTURELink trains and deploys short-term mission leaders, their teams, and career missionaries to over 120 nations. Also, CULTURELink currently has its own ongoing partnerships in Costa Rica, El Salvador, Kenya, Hungary, and Romania.

ACKNOWLEDGEMENTS

I wish to thank Jackie Fullerton for teaching me the basics of authoring a book. In between playing bridge hands, she guided me throughout the process. Jackie is writing her fourth book.

I appreciate Ellen Pensky's friendship, as she was the first to read the book's draft and inspired me to keep going.

Thanks to my pastor, Bob Petterson, at Covenant Church of Naples (PCA), for encouraging me and providing writing tips and his expertise. He is on his fourth book, also.

And a special thanks to Alisha Lavender for assisting me with editing. Alisha graduated from Florida Gulf Coast University and is headed for a career in publishing.

I am so grateful for Joann Chapman, Mary Ann Lee, Terry Manley, and the many prayer partners who have petitioned to the Lord on my behalf.

INTRODUCTION

W hat's a junk? It is an ancient Chinese sailing vessel that is still in use today. Many of my adventures took place around the South China Sea, where junks in the harbor were a common sight.

As I went through trials, I often felt like I was on a river that was in flood stage and my junk was taking on water. I was sinking and feared drowning. I thought about Peter and his relationship with Jesus.

1. Jesus called Peter to follow Him and he instantly <u>obeyed</u>.

"While walking by the Sea of Galilee, He saw two brothers, Simon (who is called Peter) and Andrew his brother, casting a net into the sea, for they were fishermen. And He said to them, "Follow me, and I will make you fishers of men." Immediately they left their nets and followed Him" (Matthew 4:18–20).

2. Peter witnessed Jesus <u>providing everything</u>.

"But Jesus said, "They need not go away; you give them something to eat." They said to Him, "We have only five loaves here and two fish." And He said, "Bring them here to me." Then He ordered the crowds to sit down on the grass, and taking the five loaves and the two fish, He looked up to heaven and said a blessing. Then He broke

the loaves and gave them to the disciples, and the disciples gave them to the crowds. And they all ate and were satisfied. And they took up twelve baskets full of the broken pieces left over. And those who ate were about five thousand men, besides women and children" (Matthew 14:16–21).

3. Jesus sent them off and He went to pray. <u>God was in control</u>, and He knew they were headed for problems. It was no surprise to Him.

"Immediately He made the disciples get into the boat and go before Him to the other side, while He dismissed the crowds. And after He had dismissed the crowds, He went up on the mountain by Himself to pray. When evening came, He was there alone, but the boat by this time was a long way from the land, beaten by the waves, for the wind was against them" (Matthew 14:22–24).

4. Peter was frightened and had that sinking feeling. Jesus said <u>not to be afraid</u>.

"And in the fourth watch of the night He came to them, walking on the sea. But when the disciples saw Him walking on the sea, they were terrified, and said, "It is a ghost!" and they cried out in fear. But immediately Jesus spoke to them, saying, "Take heart; it is I. Do not be afraid" (Matthew 14:25–27).

5. Jesus told Peter to come to Him, but fear took over and Peter began to sink. Jesus was right there with Him and took Peter by the hand. Jesus told Peter to <u>trust Him</u>.

And Peter answered Him, "Lord, if it is you, command me to come to you on the water." He said, "Come." So Peter got out of the boat and walked on the water and came to Jesus. But when he saw the wind, he was afraid, and beginning to sink he cried out, "Lord, save me." Jesus immediately reached out His hand and took hold of Him, saying to Him, "O you of little faith, why did you doubt?" And when they got into the boat, the wind ceased. And those in the boat worshiped Him, saying, "Truly you are the Son of God" (Matthew 14:28–33).

Come with me as I share my personal experiences in *Up the River on a Leaky Junk*. Jesus was always there, taking me by the hand and teaching me more about God and God alone.

IN THE BEGINNING

D id you ever feel as if you're sailing along on the ship of life and you're spending a lot of time bailing out water? Sometimes you think you are sinking, but then you realize the Lord is there encouraging and sustaining you through the journey. I want to share some of the ups and downs and "near drowning" experiences I have encountered over the years.

Life was great! David and I were married in late 1981 (a second marriage for both of us). We had good paying management jobs in the corporate world. I was one of the first women hired in the 1970s by Honeywell's Building Services Division. They had been hiring engineers and teaching them sales techniques, but shifted their emphasis to hiring people with sales experience and teaching them some engineering. I spent a lot of time in Minneapolis learning about pneumatic, electronic, and electrical controls. In fact, the first February I lived in Atlanta, Georgia, I was sent to Honeywell's Minneapolis training center. As I saw cars with electrical plugs hanging out of their front grills, I learned that daffodils were blooming in my yard in Atlanta. I was one of the first women who exceeded my sales quota, and won "Man of the Quarter" twice; they then changed it to "Sales Rep of the Quarter." I won a shaving kit and gave it to my boss for Christmas.

Later I was one of the first women in that division of Honeywell promoted to sales manager, and with a name like Dava, I was listed as "Dave" when the company directory came out. David was plant-engineering manager for Anaconda Aluminum Company at that time.

We both worked hard but played hard too. We loved to golf and had a country club membership. We took golfing vacations to Myrtle Beach, Jekyll Island, and north Florida. Add in a couple of trips to the Caribbean in 1982 where we discovered common interests in sailing and snorkeling and we were living the "good life."

Then came 1983 and the day David went into work and was called in by his boss after lunch. He said they had reorganized, and David was no longer on the organization chart. That was a difficult moment for the Georgia Tech engineering graduate. As David searched for another engineering job, he learned that no one wanted a new hire over fifty years old. He didn't want to take a job that required relocation because I had a good job.

One Sunday at church, we heard a young man named Eddie Staubb speak. On faith, he had come to Georgia to start Eagle Ranch to make life better for children and their families. My heart was touched. I remember crying and telling God, "I'd like my life to count for something other than climbing on rooftops and around boiler rooms." These were some of the things my job involved in order to sell HVAC (heating, ventilating and air conditioning) services to commercial building owners.

God heard my cry, and soon I began to sense that He was not going to open another door until I walked out and closed my present door. Yikes, leave my secure job! That was scary with David unemployed. David thought I was crazy, but he said if God showed us that was His will, we would do it. We agreed to pray. During the next year, the branch manager who I reported to left, and another one took his place. We'll call the new one "Pharaoh," because he made me want to leave Egypt. About a year later, I turned in my company car and left my corporate job, never to regret it!

I had no idea what I was going to do. The next Sunday at church, we heard another missionary speak who was home on furlough. He told us that his wife was getting a counseling degree at Georgia State University. I thought, "Maybe that is what I should do."

Monday morning came and I was ready to go do some errands and check out the counseling program at Georgia State. I can't really remember how it happened, but I found myself leaning against the kitchen counter with one of Dr. Charles Solomon's books in my hand, *The Ins and Out of Rejection*. A funny thought passed through my mind: "Look in the phone book for Grace Fellowship." I thought that was ridiculous, since they had only one counseling center and it was in Denver.

Grace Fellowship was founded by Dr. Solomon. In 1976, when my first husband left me, I wanted to crawl in a corner and die. One Sunday, my pastor gave me a copy of Dr. Solomon's, *Handbook to Happiness*. After reading that book, I went to Denver for counseling at Grace Fellowship.

Again, the thought came: "Look in the phone book for Grace Fellowship." I did, and was surprised to find that there was a Grace Fellowship office in North Atlanta. I called and went up to talk with them about counseling courses. I took their three-day and five-day seminars and completed their eight-week counseling internship.

In the meantime, David had found a job. Well, a job paying five dollars per hour. He had taken a job earlier with a company doing telephone sales, but quit when asked to lie to customers. He wanted a job where there was integrity and honesty, and one that he didn't have to work on Sundays. He let the yellow pages do his walking and found Joshua's Christian Bookstore. When he called, he spoke to Bob, the regional manager, who answered and asked him to come in to talk. David got the job.

After I completed the counseling internship, I wondered, what my next step would be. I called a Christian counseling center and talked with the founder. A few years later, he told me that he often received calls like mine and typically his assistant fielded them. He had no idea why he talked with me. He agreed to see me, and when he heard my story about leaving the corporate world and being led to the internship, he had a suggestion: form a nonprofit corporation (and he gave us a copy of his documents to follow) and then write a seminar on our "Identity in Christ." We followed his advice and got government approval for a nonprofit corporation called Just As I Am. We wrote the seminar and did seminars in churches for the next eighteen months.

By this point, we were using our corporate savings to support ourselves, along with the five-dollar-per-hour job and some secretarial temporary assignments. We thought that doing seminars was what we would be doing for the rest of our lives. But God never seemed to let us get too comfortable, and another door began to crack open.

During those months, we started attending First Baptist Church Atlanta, which had 14,000 members and was pastored by Dr. Charles Stanley. After attending FBCA for a few months, we heard an announcement about a Sunday evening training program. David, having been brought up in a Southern Baptist Church, thought it was the "Old Training Union," a forty-five-minute Sunday evening program. Sunday evening came and we went to the orientation. The course was called "Perspectives of the World Christian Movement" and we were surprised to learn that it was three or four hours per week for seventeen weeks. As the evening progressed, our hearts were touched by the speaker telling us that the Lord's heart is to reach the world for Jesus Christ. I even wept as I listened to the details of the course. We knew we were in the right place at the right time. The hindrance was that we did not have the money to pay for the course. That was soon solved when our director of World Missions offered to waive the fee. Now we just needed to buy the textbook. David went in to work the next day at Joshua's and mentioned the course to his manager, Bob. Bob told David that he had taken the course in seminary and David could have his used textbook. It was clear that the Lord was pushing us towards this course.

I was unemployed at the time and trying to get temporary secretarial assignments. The Lord seemed to arrange lots of time to study "Perspectives" while I waited on a call from the temp agency. The course brought in guest speakers, and the one that made the greatest impact on me was Elisabeth Elliot, a Christian author and speaker. Her first husband, Jim Elliot, was killed in 1956 while attempting to make missionary contact with the Auca Indians of eastern Ecuador. She wrote *Through Gates of Splendor,* published in 1957 which recounted the ill-fated mission of her first husband and four other Americans. Elisabeth Elliot returned to Ecuador with her toddler daughter to preach the Gospel to the Indian tribe that had killed her husband. She told our class that if she had waited to have pure motives for doing something, she would never have done anything. It made me realize that if we sense God directing, we had better obey Him and not try to internalize reasons for our action.

That was a life-changing course. We were ready to hit the mission field. We heard about Operation Mobilization (OM) having a couple of ships that went around the world providing Christian leadership training and material to those in less abundant countries. We applied but we were turned down. They didn't really need American Christians our age.

The director of the Missions at FBCA suggested we go on a three-month short term to Toronto, Canada. How could we go? We had a house with a mortgage that needed to be paid. He persisted, "You need to make a commitment to go and let the Lord take care of the house." We knew he was right, so we prayed with him and committed to go.

Three weeks before we were to leave, he called and said that there was a missionary family coming home for furlough from Papua New Guinea who needed a house. Would we rent it to them for a year? A year! We were only going for three months. The Lord wants us to walk by faith and not by sight; God must have had a plan for us for a year. "Well, okay, Lord, I'll go, but you have to do it all for me," I prayed.

The OM Training Conference ended on June 10, 1987. What a blessing it was—tears, cheers, praise, and worship. Our son, Craig, left the same day for a summer mission trip to Alaska. It was tough to say good-bye knowing that when he returned in September we would be in Toronto with OM on their "Turning Point" outreach project. We were not sure when we would see each other again. Yet I felt such gratitude to the Lord for rescuing Craig: five years before we were taking him to a drug rehabilitation facility. What a miracle God had done in Craig's life rescuing him from drug addiction. God's redeeming power is awesome!

It was a double miracle that I was heading for the mission field. I was not quite seventeen when I got married the first time. I was looking for someone to love me. By the time I was twenty-five, I had three sons. I did not have a role model of what a good wife and mother should be like, so I tried to do what I thought was right. Then, God intervened!

We had a young family and a limited budget. Our monthly entertainment was getting together with four couples we knew from high school. We took turns having each other to our homes. I recall one of the nights when we took a break from cooking and we all went out for dinner. We were waiting in the cocktail lounge for our table, our friend Carolyn, was telling us about a new church she was attending. Now that I look back, Carolyn had been one of those silent Christians since I knew her. She had gotten saved when she was a teenager, but now a new Bible-preaching church had fired her up. She went on and on and asked us all to come visit her church. We finally agreed to go, just to shut her up. We visited her church and all I can remember is a visiting missionary saying (or did my unsaved heart only think he said) that he even took his son to church when he had the chicken pox. I remember thinking that was ridiculous, and I decided I'd never go back.

Monday evening came and there was a knock at the door. It was the pastor of that church. After a lengthy visit, I prayed and asked Jesus to come into my heart as Savior (April 14, 1969). I was thirty, and my husband was thirty-three. He also made a profession of faith, and we were both baptized. We attended church every time the door was open, and my husband became a deacon. The church was reaching the area with the salvation message, but was a very legalistic church. We had been saved out from under the Law, and now we had to learn new laws.

Then came something that I least expected: divorce. I didn't plan it that way. When my husband left in February 1976, I was devastated. During the next days, I was numb. All I knew to do was pray.

My pastor knew of my pain and gave me a copy of *Handbook to Happiness* about the Exchanged Life. Now I realize I did not really understand the book, but I believe it got me going in a direction. The book spelled hope to me. Dr. Solomon had a Christian counseling ministry and his only counseling center was in Denver. I saw this as a way of getting my husband back. I called and made a reservation for counseling. If I could go there and change, perhaps my husband would come back. I flew to Denver and stayed in a motel within walking distance of Grace Fellowship. On April 1, 1976, I started counseling with Lee LeFebre. As I walked out of the motel and looked up at the mountains, God planted a verse in my heart.

Isaiah 55:12 states, "For ye shall go out with joy, and be led forth with peace; the mountains and the hills before you shall break forth into singing, and all the trees of the field shall clap their hands." I was to learn that victory and joy always go together.

Fast forward. No, he never came back and we were divorced. Only a few months before the divorce, I landed an outside sales job with Honeywell and they provided me with a company car. As a single mom, I did not have the financial resources to support a house and three sons even with a small monthly child support. Carolyn's husband had always been good with finances, so I sought out his advice. After reviewing my income, child support, and expenses, he showed me the amount I was short. God provided! I went into the office on Monday and received a raise in that amount, and over the next few years God tripled my income. God took up my cause.

By 1979, I was working full-time, caring for a home with three boys, and even taking courses at Rochester Institute of Technology. I was married so young that I never felt I had been single; here I was for the first time in my adult life, single. I didn't feel like I belonged with either the single group or the married group. I was living in the same house and had the same job. My Christian friends would often say, "We want to have you over," but few did. When I went to my legalistic church, I felt like I had the plague. I just didn't fit anywhere.

An employment agency put my résumé out and Westinghouse picked it up. On my fortieth birthday, I accepted a job as the first female salesperson with their air-conditioning service division. After training in Virginia, I drove to Atlanta for a time of house hunting and to begin my new job. I had arranged to meet with a realtor, and she picked me up at the hotel I was staying at. We spent the day looking at potential homes. One of the places we looked at was a condo owned by a lady named Billy. She was a Christian single mom, and we just hit it off as instant friends. She asked where I was staying and I told her. She exclaimed, "Oh no, they are having a Wiccan convention in that hotel this weekend. You better stay with me."

I accepted her invitation and spent the night. The next morning, her realtor came by. I told her what I was looking for, and she said she would look around. She went out in the Main Street Community in Stone Mountain and noticed a man sweeping his sidewalk. She asked if he might know of any places for sale, and he said he had been thinking of selling. You guessed it!

That is the townhouse Craig and I moved into. We bought a place that wasn't even officially for sale.

Westinghouse moved me and my youngest son to Atlanta, Georgia. The other two boys, who were in college and played hockey, did not want to move to Georgia.

Again, I was to learn to trust the Lord. My six-month review went well, and we all laughed as the regional manager said, "Guess we will keep you around another six months." Three weeks later, the headquarters did their end-of-the-year cuts and eliminated my job. Here I was hundreds of miles from home, a ten percent interest rate on my mortgage (the 70s were pretty bad), a few hundred dollars in the bank and no job. My old boss with Honeywell up north offered me my job back. I asked him for some time to think about it. I prayed, I cried, I prayed, I cried. Westinghouse had let me keep my company car for a month and I hit the employment agencies. Not many companies hire sales people in the month of December. I learned from one agency that Honeywell had an opening, and I ran right over there. I got in on the tail end of their interviewing process and was hired back for the same job with the same division. Company car also! Little did I know at that time how the Lord was going to continue to bless.

I was assigned to the west side of Georgia and part of the city of Atlanta. Through this assignment, I met the most wonderful man, David, and we were married in November, 1981.

TURNING POINT

2

The house is leased for a year, and off we go to spend the summer of 1987 on a three-month mission assignment with Operation Mobilization's outreach to Muslims, Hindus, and Sikhs. Toronto, here we come! The name of the outreach program was Turning Point, and was comprised of sixty teams in Europe and five teams in Toronto.

We had been assigned to a team with two single guys: one French Canadian, the team leader, and the other from Ontario. There were three single girls: one from Newfoundland, one from Prince Edward Island, and another from Detroit. We were the only married couple and the oldest among the team. A couple who had gone away for the summer allowed OM to use their home to house our team.

We sometimes laughed when we thought about coming from Georgia in the Southern USA to minister here in the north. We had envisioned a cooler summer than we were used to in Atlanta. After two days of over a hundred degrees and no air-conditioning in the house, we were melting. Not only was there no air-conditioning, but our bedroom window was small and covered by vines that grew over the outside screen, limiting the airflow. One night, we got up about midnight and sat in the car to cool off. After a week, the heat wave broke and we enjoyed the cool, Canadian air.

Our schedule was a busy one. Our training was held at The Peoples Church, a great mission-minded church. Each morning we went to the church at 7:15 for breakfast, then an hour of worship, followed by two hours of training and lectures. The training was on the East Indian culture and religions. We learned about Islam, Hinduism, and Sikhism taught by professors from the Ontario Bible College, local pastors, and missionaries, some retired and some home on leave. Following lunch, we returned to our home for a rest and prepared to leave by 3:30 p.m. We spent at least four hours doing evangelism throughout the immigrant-filled areas of Toronto. After an evening meal, which was prepared by a local church, we returned to our team home around 9:00–10:00 p.m.

The training was eye-opening, and going door-to-door among the immigrants brought interesting people into our lives. Our outreach target groups were immigrants (about 125,000) from the Indian Subcontinent (India, Sri Lanka, Pakistan, Bangladesh) and Indians from African countries, such as Tanzania. We were supplied with Gospel tracts written in many different dialects of the Indian language.

We were getting an education about peoples of the world we had never heard about nor thought about. We didn't know any of these languages and had difficulty recognizing which tract to give out. I remember standing on the edge of a large shopping center's parking lot with a heavy purse filled with tracts. This was the pathway that a steady stream of immigrants took from their high-rise apartments to the stores in the plaza. We would greet them with a warm "hello" and smile, then hold out a selected variety of tracts in our hands and say, "Pick your language." God uses the "foolish" things of the world to "confound" the wise.

Our first assignment was in a park, and I stood next to the path and reminded God, "Okay, Lord, I showed up, and you promised to do the rest." Suddenly, right in front of us, a lady stopped and put down six bags of groceries and rested. We offered to help carry her groceries home and learned that she was a Christian from Jamaica.

As we returned back down the path, we noticed three ladies in saris sit down on the grass. As we approached them, I practiced my Hindu greeting, *"No Mesta."* They laughed at my poor pronunciation and invited us to join them. We learned that their husbands were all vice consuls in the Indian consulate in Toronto. We talked about getting together again to share an Indian meal. We exchanged phone numbers, said good-bye, and as we walked away, we silently prayed that they would call us later.

Our training class took a field trip to a Hindu temple. We were all told to remove our shoes and leave all leather objects outside. I remember how depressing it was to see the grotesque plaster of Paris images on the altar of their idols: monkey and elephant gods.

I thought about Acts 17:24–27: "The God who made the world and everything in it, being Lord of heaven and earth, does not live in temples made by man; nor is He served by human hands, as though He needed anything, since He Himself gives to all mankind life and breath and everything. And He made from one man every nation of mankind to live on all the face of the earth, having determined their allotted periods, and the boundaries of their dwelling place, that they should seek God, and perhaps feel their way toward Him and find Him. Yet He is actually not far from each one of us...."

And Genesis 11:6–8: "And the Lord said, 'Behold, they are one people, and they have all one language and this is only the beginning of what they will to do. And nothing that they propose to do will now be impossible for them. Come, let us go down and there confuse their language, so that they may not understand one another's speech.' So the Lord dispersed them from there over the face of all the earth and they left off building the city." Did you ever wonder why we have so many different cultures speaking so many different languages?

The day in the park when we met the three Indian ladies kept coming up in my mind. I had a special feeling about one of the ladies; let's call her Nara. I made several attempts to call her, only to get her two sons and her husband. She was always resting or not available. One day, when I called, I got Nara and thought we had arranged for her to call back the next day to set a date to get together. The call never came. I really wondered how we could get back together again.

Our team had been praying to get into some large apartment buildings in the area. We wanted to go door-to-door among the immigrants with a survey our evangelism training had suggested. We were headed to this particular area to ask permission of the building superintendent. David and I were bringing up the rear as we walked across a street with our team. We stepped up on the curb at the same time a man from India walked by. We greeted him with *"No Mesta."* Again our pronunciation got a laugh, and he asked if we had been to India. We said, "No," and he suggested we should go because it is beautiful. He inquired if we liked Indian food, and we explained that we had never had any. He said we must come to his house for dinner the next night. His name was Sam, and he and his wife were interpreters for Immigration. Just like the Lord! Here was a complete stranger inviting us to have dinner at his home, not only us, but our whole team.

While we had been talking with Sam, two of our team members had sought permission to survey in one building and been rejected. When they told us which building they had been refused entry into, we shared with them that we had all been invited to dinner the next evening in that building. We learned later from Sam that Nara lived upstairs from him. We have a small world and a big God. "He who calls you is faithful; He will surely do it." (1 Thess. 5:24).

Our team members encouraged David and me to talk with the superintendent about surveying in all the buildings. When we approached George, the superintendent, he said, "No." We engaged him in conversation, and suddenly he changed his mind and told us we could go into certain buildings. Then he told us, "Oh, well, you can do it in all buildings, but just don't upset anyone so they call me." We said we would check back with him and he told us that would not be necessary; we were to go survey them all. We now had access to three hundred apartments with forty percent East Indian occupants and the rest Chinese, Korean, etc.

The next night, our whole team went to Sam's house for dinner. We met his wife and two children. All he wanted to talk about was God. He said that he could tell when he met us by the look on our face that we would want to talk about God. He was a Hindu, Hare Krishna, and had gone to a Catholic school in India. The meal was a variety of Indian dishes, mostly hot and some inferno. We had learned in cross-cultural communication class that we should eat what is offered and not offend. David was so good at that! The rest of us had a difficult time getting down the spicy foods. The girls on the team kept slipping their unwanted food onto David's plate. I think he ate for the whole team.

We sensed God's providence in this new relationship and invited Sam and his family to come next week to our house for dinner. I expressed a desire to get to know Nara better, and Sam volunteered to call and invite her and her husband to come with them. Again I was reminded of "Okay, Lord, I showed up and you promised to do the rest." Often we take plans into our own hands, strategizing, manipulating, only to have God reveal His *true* strategy. This looked like His way of us getting in touch with Nara.

Several days later, as we walked toward Sam's building to confirm our get-together for dinner, there was Nara, sitting on the grass. She greeted us, and we hugged each other. She said she was coming to our house on Friday. I was encouraged to trust Him more and my own smarts and resources less. I was slowly learning to "trust Him where I could not trace Him." (I heard this quote somewhere, but cannot remember where to give the credit).

On Friday, I was busy preparing dinner for our new Indian friends. I thought spaghetti, salad, bread, and a dessert would be good to serve. I had everything prepared except cooking the pasta. David had promised to pick up Sam, his wife and two children, and Nara and her husband around 7:30 p.m. There was a storm brewing, and around 6:45 p.m. David and I were sitting on the loveseat with our backs to the picture window. We were praying about the evening. All of a sudden lightning struck next door. There were splinters of tree trunk all over the yard and we could see a cloud of white smoke drifting by. We later learned it hit a tree, followed a clothesline into the neighbor's house, and blew out their TV. We now had no electricity, guests were coming, and our stove was electric.

David left shortly to get our guests, and I walked outside to survey the damage, wondering if a neighbor might have a gas stove. I saw a door open next door and knocked. They had a gas grill, and when David returned with our guests, I was cooking the pasta in the driveway. I had candles glowing in the house. As we started to serve the children, the lights came back on. Nara arrived with flowers for me and a lovely butterfly-shaped ring. When the rest of the team came home, they took the children out on the front porch and played with them. Later, they joined with our guests, played the guitar, and sang Christian songs. We felt bonds of friendship forming.

We had been supplied evangelistic tracts in various languages of India, Pakistan, and other Indian subcontinent countries. We used the dining room table for the piles of tracts and handout materials. Before our new Indian friends arrived, we had moved everything off the table to a long buffet. During the evening, we noted that Nara walked over and took some of the tracts. As the evening progressed, each guest did the same. They never said a word or asked if they could take them. We had never offered them or suggested they take any; it was the Lord doing it all. Later, our team praised God and laughed that our guests were even "stealing" tracts.

Seeds were planted, and more planting followed. We found a desire to talk about God among the immigrants in Toronto. We had dinner at Nara's and met some of her friends and business associates. Reg and Kara had just come to Toronto a week before. We stand amazed at how God opened up the conversation to Jesus and the Bible. Another time, David and Dr. Paul talked about God and their individual beliefs. So many Americans say they don't talk about religion or politics, but not so with the rest of the world.

I remember sitting among a group of Indian ladies, some young and some older. They were chatting away in their language, and I passed out Gospel tracts to them. The Lord continued to give "open door" opportunities. Nara introduced me to Aditi who was expecting a baby any day. She asked Nara to bring me to visit her when she had the baby. When the baby was two days old, David and I, along with one of our team members and Nara, went to the hospital. David met Aditi's husband and some of the other men in the family. Nara introduced me as her "friend."

When the baby was three weeks old, Nara took me to Aditi's home for a visit. When I inquired about a smudge or mark on the baby's forehead, they explained that it was to keep the "evil eye" away. Aditi's mother-in-law had come from India for the birth of the baby. I was able to give her a Gospel tract in Gujarati, which she sat reading intently. Later, Aditi accepted a tract in Hindi. We were able to give Sam's wife a Bible in English and her children a book and cassette tape about God. The next time we saw Aditi's mother-in-law, she said something in her language, which Aditi translated as, "Do you have more of those books?" We gave her some more, as well as a Bible in Gujarati. We gave Aditi a Bible and a copy of the Gospel of John. This turned out to be the day that Nara asked for a Bible in Hindi. We had been praying for an opening to give her one. Again, He did it all for me.

The girls on our team, Nara, and I went to the Indian shopping area together. Nara spoke to the shopkeepers regarding our buying needs and appeared to be a queen escorting her court around the Indian community. Nara told us that her brother in India knew Christ. As she talked about him, it appeared that he may have been saved about a year ago and attended a Christian church. She said that her father used to read the Bible. She planned to read the New Testament, and we suggested she start with the Gospel of John.

Communication was always a challenge. Nara invited us over one Sunday, and we said we could come after church. Thinking that it was for dinner, we arrived to find it was not. We munched on a few hot Indian snacks. A couple of weeks after that experience, Nara invited us again. We ate before we went, and you guessed it, she served a large Indian meal.

We had the most exciting summer of our lives. I guess we always think that evangelism and missions will be drudgery, but God sure had made it fun. At the end of the three-month outreach, we had talked with many and given tracts to even more. But there were a few friendships developed that were special like Nara and Mark, a Hungarian refugee.

We met Mark one night as we were walking through the hallways of one particular apartment building. There seemed to be no one home that evening and David commented that God must have something special for us coming up. The next door we knocked on was Mark's. He was from Hungary and had been in Canada for two years. He fled Hungary on a tourist visa to Austria where he asked for asylum and spent nine months in a refugee camp. While there, a Canadian missionary gave him a New Testament. He had been an electrical engineer in his native country, but was happy now to have a job as an electrician's assistant in Canada.

Mark invited us in and shared that his wife and eight-year-old son were trying to come to Canada. They had made four attempts, yet there was always a holdup. The latest report was that they were supposed to arrive in two weeks. Mark asked us to pray for their safe arrival.

Mark told us he was brought up believing that God was a fairy tale, but now he believes there must be a God who created everything. He brought out his New Testament and we talked about Jesus and eternal life. We asked him to ask God to reveal Himself and suggested he read a portion of the New Testament daily. We invited him to come for dinner on Sunday. We left praising God for this mission experience in Toronto. At that time, we could not freely go into Hungary and witness to someone like Mark. What freedom and opportunities we have been given in North America!

A few weeks later, Mark's wife and son arrived in Canada. She spoke a little English, but the little boy didn't know any of the language of his new country. Canada had a liberal immigration policy, and many were seeking new lives in a free land. We were told by a woman who worked for one of the government agencies that a nearby junior high school had ninety-four ethnic groups speaking seventy-four different languages. What a challenge for the teachers of these new Canadians!

WHAT'S NEXT, LORD?

3

Three weeks before our short-term mission project in Toronto came to an end, we were wondering why the Lord had us lease our Atlanta home for a year. What did He want us to do for the next nine months? One of the instructors we met at The Peoples Church was Howard Dowdell, director of the Canadian Centre for World Mission (CCWM). Howard began to talk with us about assisting him with a pilot project in Toronto.

For years, the Canadian church had been involved in world missions. They prayed for missions, gave funds for missions, held annual world mission conferences, and sent missionaries out from their congregations to serve around the world. But 1987 was a different story. The immigrants and refugees had moved into their neighborhoods, and the average Christian wasn't so sure he or she wanted to live among the mission field.

We agreed to stay on in Toronto and work with CCWM on the Barnabas Project. Howard's local church agreed to team up with us. We were to live among the immigrants and involve church members in various evangelistic activities. The vision was that if Christians sat with immigrants over a meal, they might see that we all have the same needs. Hopefully they would then reach out in friendship and earn the right to share the Gospel with these new Canadians.

We learned that we could stay an additional month in the OM team home. This would give us time to find an apartment and develop the pilot project plans further. In the 1980s, Toronto had restrictions on apartment rental rates, which discouraged the building of more apartment buildings. Thus, apartments were hard to obtain. We had committed to stay on in Toronto for a year and we needed an apartment. We felt God wanted us to be in the Thorncliff Park area, where there was a large immigrant population living in four twenty-story buildings. This was the same area we had done door-to-door outreach in. With the housing restrictions, to get an apartment in one of these buildings would take a miracle.

You'll recall that when we were involved with the OM three-month short-term team, we wanted to do evangelism in those buildings. But first we needed to get permission and met with the building superintendent, George. We later learned George was a Christian and attended The Peoples Church. George had given our OM team permission to go door-to-door. Now we wanted to live there for a year.

Our friend Maria, a member of Howard's church, lived in one of the buildings and offered to take us to the leasing office. The three of us were disappointed when we learned that there were no apartments available. We asked if we could be put on a waiting list, and the lady in charge said there was no list. As we left the building to head back to Maria's, we ran into George. He remembered us and gave us a warm greeting. When we told him about trying to rent an apartment and what the lady in the office had said, he exclaimed, "Well, I can put you on the list." He asked David for his phone number and said he would get back to us. Before the day was over, we had signed a lease for an apartment.

Learning experiences were plentiful with the Barnabas Project. The project's objective was to develop a practical and effective ministry to new Canadians, primarily and initially with East Indians within a five-to-ten mile radius of the partner church. Through cultivating in-depth friendships, it was anticipated that bridges would be built that would enable the Gospel message to be carried across the gap of cultures, background, and religion.

Church members were encouraged to become personally involved in building bridges of communication to new Canadians who had not yet been reached by the Gospel message. The ultimate purpose of the project was to win people to Jesus Christ. Through hospitable outreach and warm Christian fellowship, it was anticipated that small groups would develop that prayed and took initiative in cross-cultural outreach to the unchurched new Canadians.

During the summer, we had met about one hundred immigrants, and a few made lasting impressions on us. Mark and Anna, the Hungarian couple we met during the summer outreach, invited us to their home for dinner. They had been to our house several times and wanted to entertain us. Before dinner, Mark had us stand and hold hands and asked David to say grace. We had a wonderful dinner and lots of good conversation. Anna's English was progressing.

Harry was from Tanzania and lived with his mother, brother, and sister. Their father had died two years earlier in Tanzania. The family was Ismaili Muslims and had previously owned a garment manufacturing plant in Tanzania. I imagine they were well-to-do, but the government took the plant over, and they had to flee the country. They were now living in a sparsely furnished apartment. The mother was a lovely lady, probably in her mid to late forties.

We were also meeting new friends. While we were talking with a resident of one of the buildings, a police officer came to the door investigating an assault which had happened the night before. Along came Julia, the building manager, to see the family of the person who had been assaulted. We learned that Karna, a Tamil from Sri Lanka, was beaten and in the hospital in a coma. Later, we went to the hospital in support of the family and met Juliana and Frances. They had only been in Canada a month. Well-educated, they'd had good jobs in Sri Lanka; in fact, Frances had worked in the Ministry of Agriculture. They had to flee because of the fighting there. Nazir, an accountant by education, fled from Tanzania and now sold waterbeds.

Jamal, a refugee from Afghanistan, had been attending our partnering church and recently moved into a nearby apartment. We invited him to dinner, along with some of his new neighbors, who happened to be Muslim. He stated that he did not want to come because he did not want to meet any Muslims. He related his fears and bad experiences. He said that the Muslims talk at the mosque, and that they would make trouble for him because he attends a church. He said they had tried to get him to come to the mosque, and later he had problems with his mail being taken from his mailbox. We knew that if one is converted to Christianity in another country, that person may be killed. He was afraid, and we couldn't blame him, even in a free country like Canada. We later learned from his brother that he was badly beaten by Muslims when they learned he was a Christian, and he spent fifteen days in the hospital.

There seemed to be an assumption among the church folks that immigrants were poor, uneducated people who were interfering with the normal Canadian lifestyle. We found that most of the immigrants came to Canada with skills and qualifications, looking for opportunities and a better life. The United States was built by immigrants seeking religious freedom, and I believe many new Canadians were seeking the same.

We would hear comments from Christians participating in the pilot project like, "How long are they going to wear those silly saris?" Sometimes, I got the feeling that the local Christian was more interested in westernizing the immigrants than evangelizing them. Another said, "I wish they would just pave the whole Middle East with blacktop." One well-meaning lady who wanted to take a food/clothing package to a particular family said after meeting the family: "They don't seem to have financial problems; they drive a nice car and seem very well-educated." Another told me that her view changed after having dinner at our apartment with some immigrants. She said she was resentful about so many immigrants coming to Toronto. She says now she has gained a better understanding of their problems in their home countries and why they came to her country. She said, "It opened my eyes to how much they are like us."

Many new Canadians were Muslims, and I saw an article that said between 1990 and 2000 the Muslim population of Canada increased by 128 percent, which was the largest increase of any religious group in Canada. It said that Islam is now the third largest religion in Canada. Forty-five percent of the Muslims live in the Greater Toronto Area. The Canadian Census also showed the median age of the Muslim community was twenty-seven. The Canadian Muslim community is the most educated, affluent, fastest growing and youngest community. All signs indicate that this community will increase in political and economic clout. We went to a local printer one day to get a price on printing the Barnabas brochure. He said that he recently had another religious organization getting some newsletters printed and handed us a copy. It was an Islamic publication stating that they envisioned someday having a Muslim Prime Minister of Canada.

This pilot project in 1987 had the potential of reaching the Muslim immigrants for Jesus Christ. We were encouraged by the few church members who got involved with the immigrants and had their world view expanded. But many times we were disheartened at the lack of interest among the evangelicals to reach the world that had been brought to their shores. It was so much like the accounts in the Old Testament: when God's people did not reach out, God brought the foreigners to their land. A few years later, when we served on a project overseas to reach Muslims in a Middle East country, we couldn't believe the indifference we felt from the American church towards the Muslims we were trying to reach. One of our mission leaders was in the USA trying to raise interest for the Narnia Project. He met with a pastor in Florida and was sharing the vision to penetrate this particular Muslim country with the Gospel. The pastor said, "What makes you think that I want to reach Muslims? I don't care if they go to hell."

One way we brought church members together with the immigrants was at the Friday Night Supper and Bible study in our apartment. The large oval wooden headboard for our bed was designed so that we could put it on top of our dining room table, expanding the seating room from six to twelve.

We invited Mark and Anna to come to the supper and Bible study. Others accepted our invitations, and it grew each week. Some of the church members partnered up with us and provided food. Others came to wash the dishes. There were some very memorable moments, not always positive. I remember one night David had made an apple crisp, and when it was baked, he put it on top of the stove. Later the burner underneath was turned on and all of a sudden there was an explosion. Apple crisp and glass propelled all over the kitchen, just moments before the guests arrived.

Another way the church got involved was to distribute tracts. Twelve people distributed nearly 1,600 tracts in the door slots of the apartments in the four buildings. This took about forty-five minutes. One evening, we invited a Hindu couple over for dinner along with a couple from the church. We asked our Hindu neighbor to bring a video on Hinduism, and we would show a Christian video. We all enjoyed dinner, getting to know each other and sharing our beliefs. Hindus believe in something like 330,000 gods and will often take Jesus and add Him to their god shelf.

We teamed up with church members and went door-to-door on our floor and invited all our neighbors to an American Thanksgiving dinner. This brought the immigrants and church members together, sharing a traditional meal and the details of the origin of Thanksgiving.

Child Evangelism began a group in our apartment. Several children attended regularly, singing songs and learning about Jesus. One day, when one of the Muslim mothers brought her daughter, I asked if she would like to come in and observe the class. During the singing, I noticed that she was singing. When she was leaving, I asked her how she knew that song. She told me that her daughter came home each week and taught her. Praise the Lord, a little child shall lead them.

We started an 'English as a Second Language Using the Bible' class at the church. One of the first weeks, two Kurds came. This was the first time we had heard of the Kurds, long before they were in the news. A Muslim from Afghanistan was coming on a regular basis and then he didn't show up. We inquired with a friend who knew him as to why he wasn't coming. We learned he didn't want to come back for the English lessons because David was from Georgia, and he didn't want to speak with a Southern accent.

Susan (Chinese) and Flavio (Brazilian) were Christians who immigrated to Canada from Brazil with their three sons. She shared that her great-grandfather had converted from Buddhism to Christianity in China through the ministry of Hudson Taylor and Inland China Mission (later called Overseas Missionary Fellowship and now OMF International). Since Susan was a new Canadian herself and could relate to the other immigrants, she was interested in leading a Bible study for women. She had experienced difficulties in her new country. Adjustments had to be made in cooking for her family. In Brazil, they ate lots of beef, which she found expensive in Toronto. She had to try new recipes that were more in line with her food budget. For many immigrants, food was a huge change. They couldn't get the ingredients they were used to in their home countries. I was to learn this personally once I began to live in other countries.

There are those lighthearted times and then times with heavier issues. Divine intervention comes in unexpected forms and at unexpected times. I awoke about 6:00 a.m. with a lady named Jean on my mind. I just had to get out of bed and pray for her. She hadn't been a close friend, just an acquaintance that I had met at the CCWM office. As I prayed I began to cry and plead God for mercy for her. It was an unusual experience that morning, one I had never had before, and to date, have never had again. When I got to the CCWM office that morning, I learned that Jean had overdosed that morning and tried to end her life. She pulled through and was in intensive care at the hospital. When I visited her in the hospital a couple of days later, she opened up and asked, "How do you know if you are a child of God?" She had made a profession of faith years before, but had been trying to please God on a "performance-based acceptance." I shared that God does not base our worth and value on what we do, but on who we are in Christ. After God comes into our hearts, we are His children, His delight! John 1:12-13 says, "But to all who did receive Him, who believed in His name, He gave the right to become children of God, who were born not of blood nor of the will of the flesh nor of the will of man, but of God."

There were lean times in Toronto. We had raised support for the three-month short term. When we decided to stay on with CCWM, we did not have much financial support. Our church in Atlanta agreed to help with support. Sometimes when church members left an event at our apartment, we would find they had left some money on our table. We became the recipient of a Thanksgiving basket from the church. I remember one day we had about four dollars left, and we stopped at Wendy's. As we got out of the car, a lady in the next car said, "Do you want these coupons? I'm not going to use them." Praise the Lord!

Ernie Dyck, the associate pastor at the church we attended, was such a model of faith. He and his wife would invite six to eight people home every Sunday for lunch. They kept the menu simple with soup and salad, hoping the economical meal would be a model for others to also invite people to their homes. Sharing a meal is such a great way of getting to know each other. Some weeks at the Dyck household the finances were mighty slim. One particular week, it was a financial crisis. Ernie's wife asked what they were going to do about Sunday lunch. Should they just not invite anyone this week? Ernie said he felt they should and that the Lord would provide. On Saturday morning, they opened their door to get the newspaper, and there was a bag of groceries filled with plenty to feed the guests coming Sunday.

I am reminded of George Mueller, who lived in the 1800s. Through his simple faith in God he built great orphanages, covering thirteen acres on Ashley Downs, Bristol, England. When God put it into his heart to build these orphanages, he had only two shillings (fifty cents) in his pocket. Without making his wants known to any man but to God alone, over seven million dollars were sent to him for the building and maintaining of these orphan homes. Near the time of his death, there were five immense buildings of solid granite, capable of accommodating two thousand orphans. In all the years since the first orphans arrived, the Lord had sent food in due time. A couple of Mueller's memorable quotes are, "The beginning of anxiety is the end of faith, and the beginning of true faith is the end of anxiety"[1] and "Be assured, if you walk with Him and look to Him, and expect help from Him, He will never fail you."[2] The Bible says, "And without faith it is impossible to please Him, for whoever would draw near to God must believe that He exists and that He rewards those who seek Him" (Heb. 11:6).

One of the main things I learned during my time working on this project and trying to involve church members, was their reluctance to commit time. They were willing to do a two-hour outreach or teach an hour class, but they didn't want to commit time to build long-term relationships. Because we live in this world of instant oatmeal, fast foods, quick copies, and automated bank tellers, it appears that this attitude has filtered into the Christian community and into our evangelism efforts. Now Facebook, texting, Twitter and Instagram seem to further drive us away from building relationships that take time.

LAST MOMENT

4

Well, it was our last moment, but not the Lord's. As the year's lease on our house in Atlanta would soon come to an end and the missionary family would move out, there would be a mortgage to pay with no income. For several months, we had prayed and asked others to pray about our house in Georgia. The house was leased until the end of June, and starting July 1st, we would be responsible for the bills without the lease income. Under those circumstances, we could not stay in Toronto; we would have to return to Atlanta. We set May 30th as the date for decision. If we had not sold our house, we would then decide to go back and get jobs to pay our mortgage.

On May 30, the house had not been sold, even though we had it listed with a realtor for several months. We had to return. On June 1, we met with the CCWM steering committee to tell them we would have to leave. They decided they would keep our apartment and continue the project. That afternoon, we paid the June rent instead of giving notice. We went to the store and got some boxes for packing. As we sat having dinner, the phone rang, and our real estate agent said we had an offer on the house. A soap opera actress from New York City was marrying a man from Atlanta. At that time, twenty-five percent of the townhomes in our area were for sale. This couple came and looked at only one, ours, and put in an offer. We accepted the offer even though it was lower than we had hoped for.

We believed it was God's will and we trusted Him to make up the difference.

Now we had a new decision to make. We had to go back to Georgia and empty the house, sell some, store some, and give some away. We left Toronto on June 13 and hoped to return by August 1 to continue the outreach at least through November 1. God had other plans. Last moments sometimes turn into new opportunities to see God working. When we left Atlanta for Toronto, Craig was off to Alaska for a summer mission trip. He was now graduating from college.

When we got back to our house in Atlanta, we learned that one of the young men we knew was getting married and planning to go to the mission field in a year. We loaned a lot of our furniture to him and his new bride. Since we were going to be closing on the house soon, we had a garage sale and took the rest of the stuff to storage. We donated our refrigerator to OM. We were left with bunk beds and two lawn chairs to tide us over until closing in a couple of days. Closing delays began to happen, one after another.

Bob was opening a new Joshua's Christian Bookstore and asked David to come help. David welcomed the opportunity to make a little money while he waited for the closing. Craig came home and found the house almost empty. We told him he was welcome to choose a spot on the floor and camp out with us until closing.

When Craig learned that David was going to help get a new store ready, he asked if he could go along. Craig was planning to head for seminary soon. Bob welcomed more hands, and Bob and Craig began to get to know each other. One day Bob asked Craig if he would like a job as a sales clerk at another one of the Joshua's stores. Craig jumped at the chance for a full-time job. Craig's new manager asked Craig where he was living, and he told her the "anywhere on the floor" story. She explained that her daughter, Chris, had just gone off to college. She had a spare room. Craig moved in. Chris came home on holidays and the love bug bit. They ended up getting married. Providential? Remember when David lost his corporate job and he humbled himself to go to work at Joshua's for five dollars an hour? Was that the way God orchestrated to get Craig a wife?

Labor Day came, and our prospective buyer was getting married and going on her honeymoon. Closing finally took place at the end of September. We went back to Toronto, picked up the rest of our stuff, and returned to Atlanta.

We rented an apartment and found jobs. I got a job as a secretary in the administration/finance department at First Baptist Atlanta. David went to talk with FBCA's director of maintenance. He asked him if he had any experience with electricity. David told him that he had studied the theory at Georgia Tech and wired his house at one time. "Good! You can be our church electrician."

Henri Nouwen once said, "This is the great conversion in our life: to recognize and believe that the many unexpected events are not just disturbing interruptions of our projects, but the way in which God molds our hearts and prepares us for His return."[3]

FRIENDS FROM ABROAD

5

We got involved in FBCA's International Ministry as the Friends from Abroad (FFA) program was just beginning. It was an outreach to unchurched, unsaved international students from area colleges like Georgia Tech, Georgia State, Emory, Morehouse, etc. Most were graduate students completing their masters and doctorates. A good percentage of those who attended FFA were from Mainland China.

Friends from Abroad was held in the church's college building. FFA was envisioned to provide lunch and then break up into small groups that offered both practical and spiritual topics. The first Sunday we attended FFA, there were about thirty people there and half were church members. The international minister had hoped that one of the American couples would become the directors for the program. David and I volunteered to help and ended up directing the program.

We had been teaching English as a Second Language (ESL) using the Bible in Toronto, and that became one of the first options. Ming from Mainland China was our first student. She was the wife of a doctorate student at Georgia Tech. Dong, a professor at an area college, his wife, Lu, and their son, Ping, were some of the first at FFA. They were also from Mainland China.

The word about FFA spread, and the group grew each week. We never knew how many were going to show up. More and more students from China came. They brought their wives and children and relatives visiting from China. The Sunday afternoon program grew to 150 attending a no-reservation lunch. The volunteers helping soon numbered forty, with several who were looking at missionary careers, including Edie and her husband, Joe, and Cindy and Chuck who all ended up in China. It was truly a "fishes and loaves" experience. I tried several approaches to providing the lunch. At first, I was able to cook myself, with some volunteers helping with table setup, serving, and cleanup. Then I got the idea to ask people who came from the same country to cook a meal native to their culture. This was working pretty well, until an African group made a dish with peanut sauce. It was refrigerated and served the next day, but something happened within the peanut sauce, and we nearly wiped out all the attendees. Another Sunday, we asked the Chinese to prepare a meal. We had a difficult time trying to convince them to prepare the meal ahead of time on Saturday. Making four hundred dumplings was not going to happen early Sunday morning.

Sunday school classes were enlisted and took turns providing the food and attending to serve and clean up. They would stay and engage in conversation with the internationals. Practical programs were offered, such as learning about the American culture, preparing to drive a car, and conversational groups on current events. There were other options that had a spiritual emphasis, such as ESL using the Bible, spiritual discussion groups, and one-on-one Bible studies. With so many university students bringing their children, we began a separate children's program.

At that time, there were informers within the university who watched over the Chinese students and reported back to authorities in China. When a Chinese student began coming to a Bible class, we always gave them a Bible in Chinese. Several of these students would show up each week with their Bible wrapped in newspaper. We understood their security problems.

Thanksgiving and Christmas were lonely times for international students, especially when the other students headed to their homes to celebrate with their families. Some of these holidays, we would host dinner in the fellowship hall with church members supplying the food. Other times, we would load the students into two or three large passenger vans and drive them to host churches in Florida or South Carolina. One year on a Christmas trip, we got to the Georgia-Florida border and an ice storm had hit. David was driving one van and I the other. We were forced to exit I-75, and we inched along the icy road. We prayed our vans down a hill. We were directed to a schoolhouse, where we all spent the night.

Host churches would put the internationals up in members' homes and hold activities for the students at the church. Many of these students had not been in an American home nor seen a Christian family up close and personal. The Gospel was presented during these stays to people who had never heard about Jesus dying on the cross to give them eternal life. John 3:16 states, "For God so loved the world that He gave His only Son, that whoever believes in Him should not perish, but have eternal life."

The one-on-one Bible studies gave students an opportunity to study the Bible and ask questions in private. One student I recall was a woman named Stream. She was from Mainland China and was in a graduate program at Georgia State. She had never seen a Bible before coming to FFA. Years later, she called us one day when we were living in Hong Kong. She said that she had gone to a Billy Graham conference and gotten saved. She was passing through Hong Kong on her way to China and came to stay the night with us. Praise the Lord for people who would spend time sharing their Christian faith with internationals. Upon Stream's return from China, she came by and told us that her friend in China wanted her to come back to China and work with him. She told him she would if he built a church for her. We lost track of what happened in the next chapters of her life, but we were blessed and encouraged by her testimony.

A couple of our friends from Taiwan visited the church service. They had recently been in Los Angeles and gotten a speeding ticket. One of the requirements was that they had to return personally to pay it. That would be difficult, since they lived in Atlanta. I encouraged them to pray about it. Mey Tai called in a few days to say that her prayer had been answered, and they would not have to appear in LA, but could mail in the payment. Mey Tai had questioned me, "Who is Jesus?" I told her to ask God to reveal that to her. She came to FFA the next Sunday and was so excited. She asked God as I told her, and the answer was written in one of the little books I had given her. It was a small question-and-answer booklet written in Chinese. One of the scientists who wrote an article in the book had the same question. Mey Tai read it in her own language and that settled it, "He is the Son of God." Off she went, and a few days later she called to say she believed and had asked Jesus into her heart to save her for all eternity.

David taught the Bible to Dong and his wife, Lu. Their son, Ping, was in the children's program, learning Bible stories and singing songs about Jesus. A couple of years passed, and they told David that their nephew was coming to the USA from China to study in a college in St. Charles, Louisiana. When he arrived in Atlanta, we enjoyed getting to know him. We asked where he was going to live while he went to school. There seemed to be no plan. David and I offered to drive him to St. Charles and find him a place to live. Lu went along with us on the trip.

This was a faith journey, but we were convinced that the Lord had a Christian home for him to live in. When we drove into St. Charles, we stopped at a church to inquire if they knew of someone who had a room available. They didn't, but gave the young man a Bible. Next we stopped at a larger church and learned they had an international ministry. I called the lady who coordinated that ministry and told her that we were looking for a room in a Christian home where Dong's nephew could stay while attending college. She was very nice and asked when we would need that room. I replied, "Today." After she recovered from the shock, she said, "My son just left for college, and his room is empty. Come on over." Praise the Lord, He had provided once again.

Some of our adventures got a little messy. The four guys from Thailand who had names longer than I could pronounce wanted to cook David and me a typical Thai dinner. They came over to our apartment and dinner was wonderful, but the kitchen looked like a cyclone had blown through.

It was such a rewarding time in our lives to be used by the Lord in ministering to internationals right here at home. We had no idea that the next step would take us overseas.

MOMENTS IN MACAU

6

Our adventures in Macau took place at the end of 1990 and the beginning of 1991. How did we end up going to Macau? We were living in Atlanta and working at FBCA. One day I met David for lunch and told him that during prayer time that morning I felt the Lord might have us go to China that summer. He calmly said that if the Lord wanted him to go to China he was all for it, but the Lord would have to tell him.

We started talking about my high school friends from Rochester, NY. When I came to know the Lord as my personal Savior in 1969, I immediately wanted to share the good news with Mickey and Joe. Joe was working as a bartender at the time, and Mickey cared for their five children. One night at dinner at their home, I began explaining what the Lord had done in my life. Joe got up from the table and soon returned with his huge family Catholic Bible. We looked at scripture and they appeared quite interested, so I invited them to come to church with me. It wasn't long after that the pastor visited them and led them both to the Lord. Right away they surrendered to full-time Christian service and went off to a Bible school. The next thing I knew, they were living on a sailboat and sharing the Gospel around Singapore's small islands.

As David and I talked about their experiences, I reminded him that they were now in Macau. Macau was then a Portuguese colony (first and last European colony in China). Portuguese traders settled in Macau in the sixteenth century and it remained a Portuguese colony until the region was handed over to China on December 20, 1999. The territory's economy had been heavily dependent on gambling and tourism, as well as light manufacturing. One man owned all the casinos, a lot of the hotels, and the Jetfoils that ran across the Pearl River between Hong Kong and Macau.

"Well, David, maybe they will ask us to come over and help them." Guess what was in the mailbox the next day? A prayer letter from our Macau missionary friends ending with, "Please pray that the Lord will send American Christians to help us here in Macau." David heard from the Lord, and we began to prepare to go.

Actually, preparations had started a year before, at the time of the Tiananmen Square Massacre, also known as the June Fourth Incident in 1989. A couple in our church had been in a Beijing hotel near the Square at the time of the Chinese disturbance. They had taken some video out of their hotel window. At that time, we were directing Friends from Abroad, and we knew many Mainland Chinese students attending colleges nearby. We had gone to visit our Chinese friends on campuses and expressed our concern and prayed with these students. We organized a "Pray for China" meeting at the church. One of the ladies who attended that prayer service back in 1989 was named Lisa, a Chinese lady living in Atlanta. She told us about her auntie living in Macau. We never dreamed about going to Macau at that time.

Macau had that small-town atmosphere, with some buildings having an Oriental look while others appeared quite European. The streets were mostly cobblestone. People stopped to greet each other and no one was afraid to speak to a stranger, especially one that looked American. We were there only six months, but during that time we would meet people we knew on the streets most every time we went out. One could walk all over the country, which consisted of two tiny islands, Taipa and Coloane, and a peninsula attached to China. The country of Macau was a total of seven square miles.

With the China takeover coming at the end of the decade, people were anxious to find an immigration route to other countries. It hadn't been too many years before that Chinese had fled China and taken up residence in Macau. Those people might not have much favor with the new government taking over in 1999. Many were going to Portugal, since it was a Portuguese possession. Others who had enough money were going to Canada, mostly the Vancouver area. Chinese and Portuguese had intermarried and were called Macanese. Others wanted to learn English with a hope of going elsewhere. Our missionary friends had started a church in hopes of reaching the Chinese. Their American English School was located within the same building where they had church services. David and I would teach English classes while we were there. David, the Rambling Wreck from Georgia Tech, would teach the advanced class and I would teach beginners. We would build friendships and share the Gospel with the students.

It was agreed that we would spend six months in Macau, and now, the challenge was to get there. From Atlanta to Hong Kong was a long, long flight over the Pacific taking along several seventy-pound suitcases. Once we arrived at Hong Kong Airport, our friend Joe and his son, Caleb, met us and helped haul the luggage to the port. Once loaded onto the boat called the Fast Cat, we travelled across the Pearl River to Macau. After unload luggage and loading luggage onto a van, we were all wishing we had travelled lighter.

Macau, new sounds: Birds, singing in their cages as they were being walked like one would walk their pet dog, the drill team marching to the drum beats in the park. So many new things: the hot water faucet that won't shut off, little red bugs that come in the kitchen window (with no screens, of course), and the sink's drain that flows into a catch basin beneath the sink. New smells: a mildew odor in the halls of our building, the municipal market where the fish are displayed on countertops and the meat hangs from hooks and the Chinese pharmacy with glass jars displaying dried snake and other mysterious potions. There were so many new experiences as we settled into a strange culture. As the cars fly down the roads, dirt fills the air. Everything around us is covered in a thin coating of dust. We saw many wedding parties passing by with their decorated cars, and noticed the incense burning under trees with fruit and rice offerings to their gods. There were blind fortunetellers at little tables lined up near the post office, offering their services to guide one to success. We noticed a lot of Japanese tourists disembarking tour buses in front of gold shops. When they enter, the door is locked. I wonder if they are now captured customers. The Royal Hotel's gift shop even had some items priced in the Japanese currency.

Our missionary friends had arranged for a temporary apartment, but we needed to find one for the six months we would be there. That appeared a difficult task, since most landlords wanted a longer-term lease and large deposits. On our first evening in our temporary apartment, we were very intrigued with our new surroundings and stood looking over the back balcony. There was a restaurant just down two doors and across the street. The street appeared to be a dead-end alley. We learned that the Chinese use the building they are in, the sidewalk, and as much of the street as they want. A couple came up to the restaurant, and one of the men went down two doors and picked up a table leaning against a wall. He brought it back and set it up on the sidewalk. As we watched, we thought they must have ordered something made with eel, for the waiter walked over to a tank on the sidewalk, grabbed an eel in a net, gave a twist, and then walked to the middle of the street and gave it two hard whacks on the pavement. As they cleared dirty dishes from tables, they drained leftovers into the street and put the dishes in a pan behind a car parked in front of the restaurant. It was a taste of culture shock on night one.

One morning, we decided we would try to locate Lisa's aunt. Since Macau consisted of primarily high-rise buildings, we started walking up the street. To our surprise, nestled in between two tall buildings was a three-story single home. We walked up to the door, rang the bell, and a man answered. We explained that we knew Lisa and we were looking for her aunt. He was happy to meet us and said he was Lisa's cousin, Joel.

Auntie was a gracious hostess and served us tea. She inquired about where we were living, and we told her we had a temporary apartment until we could find one for the six months we would be in Macau. She looked at Joel, who owned several apartments and had just renovated one. He did not plan to rent it, but to keep it for his own use later. "Joel, why don't you let them stay in your apartment?" He agreed, and we now had a three-bedroom, newly renovated apartment with no lease for two hundred dollars per month.

The newly renovated apartment was not furnished, and the kitchen consisted of only a sink. We purchased a refrigerator that sat on the floor and came up to my waist. Since we needed to cook, we found a two-burner stove that sat on the counter and used propane gas. I had brought a pressure cooker from the States, so I had at least one pot. Some dishes and other kitchen items were supplied by our missionary friends and some expats they knew. I had begun teaching English to Vicky, a Chinese doctor. When she learned that I only had one pot, she insisted I go with her to her apartment. She started pulling things out of her cupboard and handing them to me. She sent me home with a teakettle, wok, pots and pans, rice bowls, a plastic pitcher, and some glasses. We saw some boards at the school and asked if we might use them. Some David put up in the kitchen to hold our dishes and three were stacked with glass bricks between to make a bookstand. Two others became a shoe rack in the bedroom. Improvise was our motto!

We had lots of room: a large living room, three bedrooms, and two bathrooms; one even had a bathtub. Oh, a bed? David built a large box that we called the bed. But he said that it could also be taken into the living room, covered with a tablecloth, and used as a table to seat a large group sitting on floor mats. He purchased a four-inch foam mattress and carried it home through the streets of Macau. We brought a small round table and folding stools home from the school.

Auntie took me shopping in the largest market in Macau. She pointed out some Chinese men who were selling meat spread on mats on the pavement. She told me, "Don't buy from them, they have smuggled that in from China and you have no idea what that meat actually is." As we walked through the market, I was able to ask about the different fruits and vegetables. It was a learning experience to watch Auntie select, bargain, and pay for her purchases. I bought my first live chicken. It was a pretty one, as the man grabbed her from the wicker basket filled with chickens. He hung her upside down and then gave me a number. After we finished shopping, we came back and picked her up. She was now dead but still warm, with no feathers, and in a bag. When I got home, I discovered that she still had her head and feet on and her heart was still in place. David took care of the extra parts. The next time we bought a chicken, we asked for those parts to be removed, and we gave them to Auntie.

One of the biggest challenges was getting our laundry done. There weren't any laundromats. We would walk over to our missionary friends (about a 30 minute walk) and do our laundry, but it took almost a whole day. We started praying that God would find a solution to this problem if He didn't want us spending a whole day doing laundry. We thought maybe we could find a lady who would take it home with her and do it, but inquiring it did not seem like a popular thing to do in Macau. We heard about a Filipino lady who would come and do it by hand, but that didn't sound so good. One night, we decided to set out with our laundry under our arms to find a solution. We had seen something that looked like Lavravia out the window. We found the place, but the lady did not speak English. She began counting our items and making out a ticket that totaled thirty-eight US dollars to have David's underwear dry cleaned. We said no; that was too expensive. A man who had been watching motioned for us to follow him. He took us down a side street to a place that looked like a laundry. They had limited English and we told them we wanted it washed, dried, and no ironing. They were dry cleaners, too. So we went back to the apartment with our dirty clothes. We started asking everyone, and finally found a tiny laundry in the back of a camera shop near the post office. We tried it, and when we got everything back we had given them, we had solved our laundry problem.

Once we got settled, we took our first trip over to Hong Kong. We had figured out how to get Jetfoil tickets to get across the Pearl River. We arrived early at the port, and David had to use the restroom. It was in dreadful condition: dirty and missing a toilet seat. There was a casino nearby, so we walked across the parking lot and went in. When we opened the door, we could tell it was a class act and immaculate. We were greeted by an attendant, who in broken English said, "Roulette?" and David answered, "No, toilet." We laughed about that for years. When we got to Hong Kong, we stopped in the terminal to buy a bottle of water and quickly learned our Macau currency was not good in Hong Kong. That was all we had in our pockets, except the return ticket to Macau. Asking around, we learned that we could get an advance on our credit card in Hong Kong currency.

When we got back to Macau, we had lots of tales to tell our missionary friends. They told us one about taking a young man named Josh to Hong Kong for his first time. Josh was from Rochester, New York, and had come as a volunteer to teach English. During their visit to Hong Kong, Josh had to go to the bathroom. They found him a place and waited outside. He was in there a long time, and they were beginning to worry that he was sick or had another problem. Well, they quickly learned about his problem when he came out with one sock missing. Josh didn't realize that in this part of the world one had to carry one's own toilet paper. We caught onto that custom real fast, and everywhere we went we had a package of tissue in our pocket.

Living in Macau gave us opportunities to visit China across the border and also travel within China very inexpensively. China was attached to Macau by a land bridge, so we could just walk from one country to the other. Checking through Macau immigration, walking across "no man's land," and going through China's immigration took less than an hour. And there we were in Zhuhai, China, and now we were fair game for the beggars. If we could just get away from the beggars near the border, we enjoyed the day. Little girls and boys were beggars. A man with a baby in his arms came begging. We later were told that the babies were drugged so they wouldn't cry. It is so sad to see these children being taught this way of life. One day, we had a persistent beggar who was practically hanging onto my arm as I walked. I had tried asking him to leave me alone, even raised my voice, but to no avail. Then I remembered once again how the Lord said, "Ask and you will receive." I simply prayed, "In the name of Jesus, go away." He disappeared as if swept away by a strong wind. Thank you, Lord.

Zhuhai manufacturing supplied many items to the USA, including some very nice handmade quilts. I purchased a couple for twenty-five dollars each and one had a New York City store's label. One was really funny, a beautiful pale blue-and-pink design with big red stars on each corner. That seemed to say it all about China at the time.

We met lots of interesting people through teaching at the American English School. Gloria was one of the students. She was divorced, with a little boy named Peter. She was a dealer in one of the casinos. We enjoyed spending time with Gloria, and she was eager to know about Jesus and the Bible. She loved music and we gave her some Christian tapes. Before long, she was singing along with Sandy Patty and other recording stars.

Gloria wanted to take us for dinner one night and raved about the ox tail she had eaten in Macau. We agreed, and the three of us walked arm-in-arm through the cobblestone streets of Macau with Gloria singing "It Is Well with My Soul." It was a tiny restaurant and the type that when they close they pull down the metal shutters that are actually the walls. To get to the seating area, we had to go up metal stairs that were over the grill, thus slippery and greasy. When we got up to the loft area and sat down, I saw a cockroach run up the wall. My stomach said, "Oh no." I remembered that everything goes better with Coke. Actually, the ox tail was delicious, but the whole experience was traumatic. A few weeks later, Gloria accepted Christ as her Savior, and the ox tail adventure was all worth it. The Bible says, "To the weak I became weak, that I might win the weak. I have become all things to all people that by all means I might save some. I do it all for the sake of the Gospel, that I may share with them in its blessings" (1 Cor. 9:22–23).

We often walked the streets of Macau, and this particular day we sat down on a bench in the town square. Along came a well-dressed man and sat down next to us. David was an extrovert who always talked with everyone. No different this day, he opened up conversation with our new friend. He told us he was an international attorney from Shanghai and was in Macau to help rewrite the laws for China's takeover coming in a few years. David asked what future changes he predicted for Macau. He said, "As long as the hen who lays the golden eggs continues to lay them and send them to Beijing, there will be no changes." What he was saying was that as long as the casinos kept producing money and a good portion of it went to Beijing, there would be no problem.

If you look at Macau since the 1999 takeover by China, you will notice how the gambling industry has expanded and has surpassed Las Vegas as the world leader in gambling revenue. Gambling breeds other vices. When we lived there, we knew that there was a prostitution ring involving young girls from Thailand. Just up the street, there was a beauty shop where they got all prettied up for their nighttime assignments. Some nights, in the wee hours of the morning, we would be awakened by noise in the street below us when the girls were returning home.

One of our first days out walking, we got lost. We had a street map of Macau, but it was in Chinese and the street signs were in Portuguese. We saw a policeman on the corner and showed him our map and asked him to locate on the map where we were. He turned it one way and another way and shrugged his shoulders. I don't think they taught map reading in this part of the world. We started carrying a card in our pocket with our address written in Chinese because the Chinese taxi drivers did not know where to take us when we gave them our Portuguese address.

Another day, we were out walking near the Chinese border when we noticed a man running through a field on the China side toward the Macau side. We actually witnessed someone fleeing from China and he made it. We had heard this happens frequently, and every week at least 150 illegal immigrants are taken back across the border to China. Someone told us some illegal vendors go back and forth on a regular basis.

Macau was filled with people from many countries. One day, we were in the church office when two young ladies, Cindy and Wanda, came in. We soon learned that they were students at the Macau Bible College. Cindy was Chinese and was born in Burma (now Myanmar). She was not sure she could return to her home in Burma, because she had been supportive of Aung San Suu Kyi, who had been put under house arrest.

Cindy's path to Jesus began when her cousin, who lived in Canada, sent her a Bible. He later sent her an application for the Macau Bible Institute, thinking she was a Christian. She went to the pastor of a church in Burma and asked him to fill out part of the application. He said, "Cindy, you are not a Christian." She told him she wanted to become one. He asked her to meet with him for a Bible study to see what the Bible had to say about becoming a Christian. She met with him and studied the Bible, learning that Jesus died for her sins, and she could have eternal life by accepting and believing in Him. She became a Christian about three years before we met. She first went to a Bible school in Hong Kong, but had to leave because of visa problems. She came to Macau to the Bible Institute on a three-month visa and was applying for a longer stay. She said she would love to go to Columbia Bible School in the USA. After I returned to the States, I heard from Cindy that she was in China, living among a minority group.

Wanda was born in Cambodia and told us that after the Communist takeover, there were many leaving on boats for Vietnam. Her brother kept telling her that she should go, but she was scared. She feared that if she went to get on a boat and did not know Vietnamese, they would send her back. Her brother had heard about a boat leaving one night and encouraged her to go with him and his family. There were guards on each side of the gangplank that they had to pass. Her sister-in-law and children got on the boat. Her brother said, "Go, Wanda." She was so afraid that she kept refusing. Finally he insisted that she go, since the boat was ready to pull out. A lady came off the boat because she had forgotten something, and when she went back to the boat, Wanda started walking behind her. As she approached the gangplank, she closed her eyes, and the next thing she knew, she heard people talking and she was on the boat. As the guards turned to say something to Wanda, her brother ran and jumped on the boat, distracting the guards. She ran into the crowd, and he did also. Before the guards could come on board the boat, it started leaving the dock.

She arrived in Vietnam, and since she was a teenager, she was expected to do hard work and was given very little food. She became sick. Her sister-in-law became a Christian soon after arriving in Vietnam. She would invite Wanda to church, but Wanda wanted nothing to do with it. Wanda was angry. Her sister-in-law would read her Bible at night, and Wanda would tell her to turn off the light just to keep her from reading it. The sister-in-law would turn it off and not argue and that made Wanda angrier. She even hid her sister-in-law's Bible so she couldn't read it. All the time, God was using this witness to win Wanda. Wanda finally went to the church and got saved, but did not read her Bible or go to church after.

Wanda's brother wanted a good future for her and talked with her about escaping by boat to Thailand. This plan took money. Another brother who lived in Hong Kong sent her ten thousand dollars to pay a man with a boat who promised to take her out. He asked for a one thousand dollar deposit, and then she never heard from him again. Her brother had a friend with a boat who said he would take her, and his mother-in-law who had a lot of gold. When the time came to leave and they had paid, he turned them into the police, and Wanda found herself in jail. The people at the church were praying for her to get out in three months. She herself was now praying and asking God to get her out of jail in three months. The normal sentence was five years. Her sister-in-law also was put in jail, but got out because she had small children. Praise the Lord, Wanda was released in three months.

She started going back to church. Since she had no money and she thought she had no hope of getting out, she started praying that God would get her to a new country. Her brother met a man who had taken his own family out by going back into Cambodia and walking through the jungles to Thailand. Her brother asked if he would take his sister out, but she had no money. The man said that was okay, he would take her any way. Wanda knew it was God answering her prayer, because God had the power, and she had no money. She went to Thailand via this dangerous route. It took her about three months, and one wrong move would have meant death.

When she got to a refugee camp in Thailand, they asked her where she wanted to go. She told them Canada, Australia, or New Zealand. She had relatives and friends in each of these places. She was asked if she wanted to go to the USA and she said she didn't know anyone there. That is where she ended up, arriving in 1980. She learned English and started attending a Chinese church. She still would not yield totally to the Lord, but was in an accident that could have been fatal. As the car was spinning, thoughts were going through her mind that she was going to be with Jesus and had "empty hands." Her face was cut badly, yet it healed without a scar. Wanda became involved in the Christian Chinese Mission and was in Macau studying the Bible. She planned to spend her life reaching Chinese for the Lord and had thoughts of going to Columbia Bible College for two years. The Christian Chinese Mission has become a sending mission organization, and Wanda is talking with them about being a missionary while in Macau. She now speaks Cambodian, Vietnamese, Mandarin, Cantonese, and English.

Meeting these two girls was a highlight of our time in Macau. We had a Bible study in our apartment with them and other Bible School students. David helped Wanda make out her USA income tax. Often the girls would stay and eat with us or we'd all go to McDonald's to have a taste of the USA.

OFF TO GUANGZHOU

A fter several months in Macau, we decided to venture further into China. We learned that we could get a bus in Zhuhai that would take us to Guangzhou, previously known as Canton. Guangzhou is located on the Pearl River and is the capital and largest city in the Guangdong Province. Since this was only a year or so after the Tiananmen Square Massacre, going into China was still a little shaky. We learned that the best way to travel safely was to work with a travel agency in Macau which would arrange for our visa and hotel vouchers.

We boarded the bus at Macau's Hotel Beverly and saw Alex, who issued our visa at China Travel. We took the bus to the border, got off, and checked through Macau immigration. Back on the bus, we were driven across the border to Chinese immigration. Then it was off again, and through immigration and customs inspection to enter China. When we came out of the building into Zhuhai, there was Joel, our landlord and friend, with a Chinese couple. Joel introduced us to Tommie, an architect from Macau, and his wife, Polly. Joel explained that they were Chinese and were married about four years ago when they met in another city in China. Tommie had a visa to Macau, but Polly couldn't get one, so she lived in Zhuhai, and he went there once a week to see her. They were still hoping that she could get a visa to Macau next year. I fell in love with this darling

Chinese lady. She invited us to visit her when we had to go to Zhuhai every twenty days in order to come back to Macau on a new visa.

Joel was like a "mother hen," watching over us. We walked to a nearby hotel, where we waited for the bus to Guangzhou. When the bus arrived, it loaded fast. We got on, and David went to the back, took a seat, and motioned for me to sit up front. Then the man next to him moved making room for us to sit together. Joel poked his head in the bus and shouted, "Are you all right?" The bus was filled to capacity; in fact, there were seats filling the aisle that had been pulled down after we loaded. It was packed, an ocean of heads in front of us. Joel, Tommie, and Polly stood outside the window with worried looks on their faces. They were probably envisioning us trapped in the back if something happened. Better we didn't know about things that had happened in the past in China. Soon the bus took off and we could see our friends waving until we were out of sight.

I had heard people tell stories and had some good laughs about the roads in China, but never until now did I realize how true the stories were. A washboard is a mild description of the shaking ride we had through small towns and larger villages. New and interesting sights passed by our window. What an adventure! We saw water buffalos in the fields, some pulling ploughs and gardens divided into small plots probably allotted to different families so they could grow their vegetables. The trees along the road were covered with dust, dust was in the air, and everything looked dull gray. Some towns we passed through had dirt streets. Before leaving, I had asked the Lord to let me see China through His eyes. My view of China so far could be summed up in two words: dark and gray.

About two hours into the trip, the bus stopped, and an announcement was made in Chinese. We assumed that it was a restroom stop, so when the seats were raised from the center aisle, we got off. I followed the ladies to a small block building and entered. Oh my, even the Chinese ladies were moaning about the smell and condition of the toilets. It had a half-wall between each toilet, which consisted of a cement trough - no flushing, either. It motivated me to go quickly and get out of there as fast as I could. Little did I know that this was the beginning of many experiences with toilets in China.

As we travelled along, everything looked like it was under construction. Even new buildings looked unfinished with building materials left behind covering the dirt piles in front. We saw some people sweeping the dirt outside their building, like people mow their grass. We knew they were occupied, as we witnessed people going in and out and saw laundry hanging from bamboo poles out windows.

We arrived in Guangzhou and were let off in front of a hotel. From Macau, we could only buy a one-way ticket, so our first concern was to find the place to buy the return ticket back to Zhuhai. We were told to go down the street to the China Travel office that would be open in fifteen minutes. We walked along, carrying our luggage and probably looked like lost sheep among the multitudes of Chinese. Men approached us frequently wanting to exchange our money, which was illegal. Then an English-speaking girl started befriending us, but we soon noticed that we were passing in front of a duty free shop and she wanted us to go in and buy a TV for her with foreign exchange currency she had gotten illegally. At that time, the renminbi was the official currency, but foreign visitors to China were required to conduct transactions with foreign exchange certificates issued by the Bank of China between 1979 and 1994. We had learned that there were special foreign exchange stores where only foreign visitors could go. The Chinese population was not allowed in these stores.

Ahead of us, all we saw was a construction site, so we walked back to the hotel, where we ran into Alex from China Travel. We couldn't help remember the Lord's promise: "It is the Lord who goes before you. He will be with you; He will not leave you or forsake you. Do not fear or be dismayed" (Deut. 31:8). We told Alex we wanted to buy our return bus ticket, so he took us outside and down the street to the "construction site." Sure enough that was where to purchase the bus tickets. Unbelievable! The area was torn up with a gangplank over a gaping hole so one could get to the building. David ventured the gangplank, and I waited on solid ground with the luggage. He came back with a big smile and two tickets back to Zhuhai. We felt more secure. Silly us! Days ahead were filled with more cultural surprises.

We got a taxi and showed the driver a card written in Chinese: "White Swan Hotel." The streets were full of bicycles and buses that looked like they would fall apart at any moment. I had dreamed of going to China one day, and here I was riding through the streets while so many strange and new sights flew by. We arrived at the White Swan Hotel, an elegant five-star hotel. It probably was the nicest hotel I had ever stayed in. What a contrast between the inside of the hotel and the outside of the real China world. The lobby was impressive, with a huge decorated Christmas tree in the center and a gingerbread church displayed.

When we arrived at the fourteenth floor, where our room was located, we noticed that it had floor attendants. They kept track of our coming and going while we were there. When we left our room, they would be right there to push the button for the elevator. Our room was lovely, with a view overlooking the city and the Pearl River. The room cost was sixty dollars per night for this luxury. I noticed a church steeple with a cross on top. Looking out the window, I remarked that the city view would look nice at night. I was wrong. At night, it was almost completely dark. Very few lights were lit in this large city.

We were anxious to get out and take a walk around the area and find the church we had seen from the window. It was not far and had a tall wall around it. The gate was never open during our stay. We walked further and found the US consulate with the American flag flying high. It was good to know they were so close. Along the sidewalks were gutters, and I wondered what they were there for. I noticed water emptying into them from pipes coming from the buildings. Yep, it was wastewater, and some noodles floated out. The area did not appear as dirty as Macau, where we were used to seeing garbage all over the streets. We did not see garbage or litter in Guangzhou. We would peer down little alleys, and they were neat.

As we continued walking, we were again approached by men wanting to exchange money. We walked along the river and watched the people loading and unloading from the ferry that ran every few minutes across the Pearl River. It was 5:00 p.m., when David noticed the end-of-the-day traffic jam. There were wall-to-wall bicycles going up a ramp to cross a bridge. It was an amazing sight. We had observed that every few blocks, we would see a lady with an armband stationed at a corner. We called them yard guards. We were later to learn that they are the area stoolies that keep track of who comes and goes in their neighborhood. That's a way of life with Communism.

We saw a hotel called the Victory Hotel and decided to check out rooms there for a possible future short-term mission team. It was cheaper and had rooms with six beds for a total of forty-eight dollars per night. It had a Chinese toilet (a hole in the floor and no seat, but it flushed). That might lend itself for a cross-cultural experience for a mission group.

We were walking along past a restaurant, and all of a sudden I was startled and moved further away. The restaurant's menu was displayed in cages, and you could choose an exotic meal. We saw two tiny deer (live and about two feet tall) sitting on the sidewalk, chained. Next to them were a couple of wire cages with large snakes and other cages with pigeons, rabbits, ground hogs, quail, and some animals unknown to me. I had the same kind of feeling the first time in Macau when I passed a restaurant and a man was sitting on the steps skinning frogs.

We had all our meals in the White Swan Hotel's restaurants. We were able to sample three of them, and the provincial Chinese was our favorite, with dishes from different parts of China. The service was great, and we got to talk with our waitresses and busboys. One waitress told us she had made the star for the top of the Christmas tree. David asked her if she knew what the star represented. She didn't, and he proceeded to tell her the story about Jesus. When we left, we gave her and the busboys Gospel tracts about Jesus wrapped in their tips.

I have to admit that as I sat there eating in this lovely hotel, I told David, "This is going to be hard to write about as a mission trip into China." We got back to our room and our beds were turned down, chocolates left on the nightstand, slippers next to the bed, and a terry robe in the bathroom. I started to feel guilty about the blessings. Maybe I had read too many stories about missionaries in the jungles living in grass huts and the hardships of missions and not many stories about material blessings the Lord gives. Perhaps there is a fear among missionaries to write about such blessings, fear that their support will stop coming. I concluded to myself that people need to hear our whole story. It was indeed a part of this mission trip. Maybe more people would be willing to surrender to the mission field if they know the Lord promises that if you are obedient He will give you the desires of your heart. Psalm 37:3–4 says, "Trust in the Lord, and do good; dwell in the land and befriend faithfulness. Delight yourself in the Lord and He will give you the desires of your heart."

We awoke early the next morning and turned on the TV. The CBS evening news from America was on. We looked out the window and the city was covered by fog. Again I thought of how dark and gray China looked to me. We showered with all the hot water we wanted to use. Back in our apartment, we had a little instant tank that we lit when we wanted to shower. We stopped at the hotel's post office, and there was a girl wearing a red sweatshirt that read "Georgia." We commented about it, and she asked if we knew where that was. We learned she attended the University of Georgia for a year, doing agricultural research. It was a touch of home. We had an American breakfast complete with pancakes. Once, we found Bisquick in a store in Macau. We were saving it for when one of our former Friends from Abroad teammates came to visit the end of January. Chuck was teaching English in China among an unreached people group.

It was easy to take a taxi from the hotel, because the doorman told the driver where to take us. One morning, we asked to be taken to Yuexiu Park. People were in the park doing the tai chi, gentle exercising, and meditation typical of Chinese. We noticed a lady carrying her parakeet sitting on its cage, and she was eager to pose for a picture. We saw groups of older men playing cards and checkers. We had a map and followed the path to the Zhenhai Tower (a five-storied pagoda), which is a six-hundred-year-old building and houses a museum on all five floors. We believe it used to be a fort protecting the Pearl River harbor. While there, we met one of the employees who spoke English well. Somehow, we got on the subject of churches, and she said she attended church. We asked her if she was a Christian, and she told us she wasn't but she liked the music.

At the end of the park, there was a tall monument to Dr. Sun Yat-sen (the founder of the Republic of China) and a sculpture of the Five Rams, which is the symbol of Guangzhou. We found Dr. Sun Yat-sen's memorial hall and took some pictures. We walked along the streets. We really stood out among the Chinese. Some would stare at us. If we caught them looking, they would look the other way. Then they would glance back to take another look. Some ventured to try their English with a "hello."

We had seen a vegetarian restaurant on the map and thought if we passed it we might eat there. No live menus for us. We thought with vegetarian, we wouldn't get snake or dog. We did pass it, but decided not to risk it and eat in the hotel instead. We continued on and found one of the oldest mosques in China, the Huaisheng Mosque with the Guangta Minaret. It was built in 627 during the

Tang Dynasty (618–907), when an Arab, Sad Ibn Abu Waggas, first brought the Koran to China. It is named Huaisheng (Remember the Sage) in memory of Muhammad the prophet. Its Guangta Minaret is quite unique, but the mosque had not been open for some time.

We did see evidence of Buddhism as we walked through the streets. There were some Buddhist shrines in a few stores with incense burning. We saw Merry Christmas and Happy New Year written in the window of one store and a few Christmas decorations scattered around here and there. Most were of Santa, but not of Jesus. One small store had a Christmas tree and decorations for sale. Most of the stores we saw were small, about six feet by six feet and did not have many goods displayed. We saw where round briquettes of carbon were being made that were used for cooking. They looked like filthy places to work, and the people in them wore facemasks. There were stores with parts for motors, electronic parts, nails, and other small hardware items. We saw jackets for sale in shades of green, blue, and gray, typical colors worn in this Communist country. I guess these colors add to the drabness I saw in China.

We got tired of walking and took a taxi back to the hotel. We rested a little while and then decided to walk to a nearby market that we had seen on the map. We walked across a bridge and down to the market entrance. It was very dark and crowded inside. I was frightened and held tight to David's arm. He had my passport and all our money and I didn't want to get lost. We walked through a long stretch with various displays of roots and dried herbs. Then it seemed to get lighter, but yet very crowded. Meats were hanging from hooks, and we recognized a roasted dog among them. We left the market area and found a department store on the lower level of a building. David bought himself a typical Chinese blue cap that we saw all the men wearing, and I found a jade cross. I was surprised to see a variety of crosses for sale. It was quite dark when we left the store, and we hailed a taxi back to the hotel. We decided to try dinner in the hotel's Cantonese restaurant.

The jade cross inspired us to go to the jade factory the next day, but soon saw that jade was very expensive. We walked through the streets observing the people and thought we would visit the Friendship Store, where only foreigners could purchase items using the foreign exchange currency. We spotted it on our map and noticed it was near a hotel called Bai Yan, in the northeast part of the city. We flagged a taxi, and David showed the driver the map in Chinese and pointed at the location we wanted to go to. The driver nodded and appeared to understand. As we were riding along, he turned to the south, and we thought maybe he was cutting south to pick up a main highway. But he went further south and we looked at each other and said, "He is taking us to the White Swan Hotel where foreigners stay." Sure enough, we ended back at our hotel, so we thought we might as well have lunch and start again. After lunch, we took a short walk past the church with locked doors and past the US Consulate with a long line of Chinese waiting outside probably to apply for a visa to the USA, and then back to the hotel. We thought we'd try again to go to the Friendship Store. This time, we had a doorman giving the directions. We had heard that they sold lots of things made in China. The local Chinese stores do not have any of these goods because they all are exported and the locals can't afford to buy them. After shopping, we realized we were in rush hour and took a taxi back to the hotel. What a ride, just like Six Flags. I was sure that the taxi was going to run over people on bicycles, and I kept ducking down so I couldn't see what was happening.

We were up at 4:30 a.m. to journey back home to Macau. We ate breakfast in our room enjoying the banana bread that our missionary friend had sent with us. We were ready to leave at 6:00 a.m., with our bus leaving at 7:00 a.m. The doorman woke a taxi driver up, and we got in after he was told where we wanted to go. The driver pulled out a ten yuan bill and showed us, indicating that would be the amount of the fare. David shook his head no and pointed to the meter, which taxis were supposed to use. The driver was so persistent that David called the doorman over and related the problem. We had heard horror stories of people being driven to remote areas and left when they would not pay exorbitant taxi fees. It was still dark, and we needed to get to the right place on time to catch the bus, so we requested another taxi. No problem with taxi driver number two, and his meter charge was 3.6 yuan.

We waited for the bus, and about 7:00 a.m., it arrived out front. We loaded, and there were only six of us going back to Zhuhai. On the outskirts of Guangzhou, we almost hit a truck that pulled out in front of us. We praise the Lord for His protection and that we were going back to Macau where there was still freedom. About two hours into the trip, David realized that this bus driver was not going to make a restroom stop. Since we only spoke about a dozen words in Chinese, we had devised the "index card system" in order to survive in China. I had been giving a doctor in Macau English lessons and asked Vicky to write Chinese letters next to some English phrases on several index cards, survival phrases like "Where is the toilet?" and "How much does it cost?" and "Where do I buy a ticket?" David pulled out the "toilet" card and flashed it at the driver. He nodded his head and in a few yards pulled into a restaurant's parking lot, only to see it was closed. After several miles through small villages, he found a gas station for another unique toilet experience.

Arriving back in Macau we were thankful for a safe trip, but not anxious to go back to China for a while. It took a few days to get over the depression we had felt in dark, gray China. To sum up our trip, we had seen a variety of toilets and had a rest in a lovely hotel, a break from ministry in Macau. We got to watch the CBS evening news one morning and eat in a good hotel. Most of all, we returned to Macau with a new determination to reach out to the Chinese in Macau and share Christ with them in a country where we had the freedom to do so. We were motivated to encourage Christians in the United States to reach out to the Chinese there.

About three weeks later, when we had to go out of Macau on a visa trip, Tommie went with us, and we visited his wife, Polly, in Zhuhai. We gave her a Bible in Chinese, and she was so anxious to read it that she walked down the street with us reading the Bible. Living in America, we have so many freedoms that others do not have. Sometimes the Bible is only used as a bookend on a shelf, and we forget that it is the living Word of God.

CHINESE NEW YEAR

8

Chinese New Year (also known as the Spring Festival) is the most important and longest holiday in the Chinese calendar. Everyone greets you with Happy New Year, "*Gung Hei Fat Choi,*" or 'May You Have Good Fortune.' The color red holds a significant place in Chinese New Year celebrations. People wear red clothes. They decorate windows and doors with red color paper designs for good fortune, happiness, wealth, and longevity. Children are given "lucky" money in red envelopes. For the Chinese, red symbolizes fire, which traditionally was believed to prevent bad luck. Two flowers commonly associated with the Chinese New Year are the plum blossom, which is a symbol of courage and hope, and the water narcissus, which symbolizes good luck and prosperity. Down at the Inner Harbor, junks are covered with lights, while firecrackers go off day and night.

To prepare for Chinese New Year, people clean their houses and sweep floors to get rid of dust and bad luck. Cleaning is meant to appease the gods who come down to earth to make inspections. They also get rid of old furniture. I'll tell you later about some good furniture finds in a dumpster.

The teachers are coming!

We first met Chuck in late 1988 at Friends from Abroad. He had just returned from three years of teaching in China. He was getting his master's degree in ESL at Georgia State. I always loved Chuck and his unique laugh. I was excited to hear that he would be coming to visit us during Chinese New Year. In the early days of Friends from Abroad, we depended on Chuck to do the program following lunch. I told him that when he came to Macau, we would have a party and let him do the program, just like Friends from Abroad. He brought Bob, who was also teaching English in China among an unreached minority group.

Chuck and Bob arrived and announced the "girls" would be arriving in a couple of days, meaning the three American women who were teaching in their locale would be joining us. We had plenty of room in the apartment, since the two spare bedrooms did not have any furniture. Now we had a girl's dorm and a guy's dorm, and all we had to do was borrow some sleeping bags, since we had plenty of floor space.

My motherly instinct was to fatten Chuck up, since he had lost thirty pounds in the past five months. Besides the rice meals he got in China, he had befriended the owner of a Muslim restaurant and Chuck taught him how to make French fries. Chuck left a bottle of ketchup on a shelf in the restaurant to use when he came in to satisfy his longing for the American staple.

It was fun showing the girls and guys around Macau. We explored the Old Protestant Cemetery, where Robert Morrison was buried. He was the first missionary to translate the Bible into Chinese. We walked along the waterfront that was always interesting, with a variety of junks bobbing in the water. People actually live on these junks, with their laundry suspended from the sides, drying on bamboo poles. We went up the hill to the lighthouse for a panoramic view of Macau and the ruins of St. Paul, now a symbol of Macau, with only the facade standing.

Before the teachers arrived, we started telling friends we would have a party at our apartment in their honor. Chuck had such a wonderful way of relating to people and getting them involved in conversation, as well as making us all roll on the floor laughing. Among the guests at the party were three young men from Beijing, who we referred to as the Three Musketeers. They were engineers from China, in Macau temporarily to work on a building project, and studied English with us. One told us that his father was a provincial leader. Chuck invited them to come over another evening and play backgammon for M&M's. When we left Macau, the three engineers had tears in their eyes. We encouraged them to continue to learn about Jesus, the only source of meaningful life. The six months in Macau was an uplifting experience, during which we saw about ten people come to know Jesus as their Savior.

Chinese tradition involved visiting your ancestral home during Chinese New Year. Auntie had embraced us into their Chinese family and invited us to go with them to their ancestral home in southern China.

Joel rented a van in Zhuhai with a driver for the week. Our driver told us he had a one-year-old daughter and really wanted a boy, but was not allowed to have another child. He said he had been driving for five years and would not get a good job if he had a second child.

The streets were full of people loading buses and vans to spend the holidays with relatives in China. It was exciting to be traveling with Chinese friends and visiting non-tourist locations. The van was large enough to hold ten of us (the driver, David and I, Auntie, her husband, her mother, Joel and his wife and two children). We headed out the same road we had taken to Guangzhou in December. Zhuhai is a Special Economic Zone and has gates where you must get approval to enter and a checkpoint when leaving. Riding in the van did not seem to be as bumpy as the bus we had taken.

Many of the towns looked familiar, since we had just been through them recently. Our first stop was at a friend of one of our companions, where they would change Macau currency into Chinese. Later on, lunch was at a charming roadside restaurant where we were escorted to a little bamboo teahouse in the back. It was a private dining room next to a pond where the "fish of the day" were awaiting our selection. Round tables with sliding windows were delicately framed with lacquered wood strips. What a special treat! We had a variety of dishes: a fish soup (not too fishy), orange-glazed ribs, chicken that we were told only ate grass and was not fatty, steamed rice, the black hair moss dish for good luck, a tofu dish, mutton, fried fish, a vegetable dish with bitter melon and an eggplant-like vegetable stuffed with seafood, steamed bread with lotus seeds, and two kinds of tea.

As we returned to the road, we were covering new territory for us. We passed green fields with little gardens where people had rented a patch of land from the government to grow vegetables. We stopped in a small town to buy tickets so we could go up to the top of Lotus Mountain (Lianhua Shan). The brochure said it is the ruins of an ancient stone mine built long before the Ming Dynasty, with steep cliffs, perilous precipices, strange rocks, and fantastic grottoes. When we got to the top, we noticed that we were the only foreigners in sight. In fact, on the whole trip we saw only three others who weren't Chinese. We were travelling among Chinese with Chinese to Chinese tourist sites where probably most Westerners never go. We were on display everywhere we went. Some people would try out their "hello" in English, and some young girls would giggle when they saw us.

We took pictures of the Lotus Pagoda but chose not to climb it. We went in the barracks of the Qing Dynasty, which was a fort with high rock walls. We were able to walk around the rim on a walkway and take pictures of the magnificent countryside. On one side, it overlooked the Pearl River, where we saw large ships anchored. There was a museum with the armor of warriors, and Joel coaxed David to sit in a carrying chair. The little Chinese man told Joel they would not be able to lift the big foreigner. By that time, a crowd had gathered to see a large American man in the chair, some getting a fast photograph of the phenomena.

Auntie's mother was the grandma on the trip, passing out cake and candy to all of us. She did not speak any English, but we had a friendship built on hugs and smiles. She told us through Auntie about the time they were both in Vancouver visiting another daughter and Auntie got lost. She said all the houses looked the same, so she went up to each door and tried her key. If someone would open the door, she would try to explain it was the wrong house.

We pulled into Foshan around five at the Rotating Palace Hotel. It might have been a four-star (sort of a rundown Holiday Inn). It only cost about thirty-five US dollars per night. Our room was very nice with a color TV. We got to watch the CBS evening news live every morning. We had a Western-style toilet and tub with hot water. The view out of our window was a mosaic of brown tile rooftops. When it got dark, there were only streetlights on the main street where our hotel was located. An occasional building had some lights strung around, and we could hear and see the flash of firecrackers exploding. Foshan was nicer than Guangzhou and not as old. The people seemed happier; perhaps it was the holiday mood. There was not much traffic on the streets, and truck traffic was almost nil because of the holiday. Taxis were few, and those that were running were the "three legged chicken" type: little three-wheel vehicles with a space for the driver up front and a tiny truck-like back with benches on each side. Most people seemed to be away celebrating the New Year. Not many bicycles and only a few vans and tourist buses were on the streets.

Auntie's husband knew the chef at the hotel. We were treated like royalty with a banquet. Our dinner was served in a private dining room, at a large round table with a lazy Susan in the middle. There was a TV blaring that I felt spoiled the atmosphere, but others didn't seem to notice. A cup of tea was served first, to get your stomach ready for the dinner. Everything is said to be "good for you" or "good for your blood" or "good for your heart." I never heard Chinese say they eat anything because they like it, but it is always good for you.

We had chicken, ham, and ginseng soup served in a beautiful hand-painted urn. I enjoyed the taste of the soup and was glad I had eaten it before they raised a small black whole chicken with its head on from the urn to show us the "black chicken." We had crab and bamboo hearts, another chicken dish, shrimp, and Chinese ham. A whole steamed fish was served, and Auntie liked the head best. We also had sticky rice, noodles, and a pigeon dish. That was our first pigeon, and it was very sweet and quite good. Small dishes of pickles and nuts were served. Before the trip was over, we were really managing well with chopsticks, even picking up a single peanut.

We left the dining room and all walked around the block. As we walked, we were stared at and pointed at. A child ran to her father, and Auntie translated that she said, "Look, that man speaks English." When we came back, while we were waiting for the elevator, the hotel hostess told us her brother lived in San Francisco, and she had a relative who was a pastor. I handed her a tract about Jesus, and the next day she greeted me like I was her best friend. This made me wonder if she was a Christian and didn't dare to say so. We are so blessed in the United States, and I felt doubly blessed to be taken on this tour with such dear Chinese people.

We were told to be ready to go by 9:00 the next morning, so we got up early and went to the coffee shop to have an American breakfast. Two waitresses hovered over us, and as soon as it looked like we might be finished with a dish, they retrieved it. Sometimes they were trying to take it before we were finished. David ordered scrambled eggs and got soft boiled. The juice was canned even though the area grew oranges. I had a treat: toast with Kraft orange marmalade. We didn't have a toaster in Macau, so I usually had fried bread. The coffee was very thick and the oatmeal was very thin. Chinese time is different than American time. We were almost finished when our Chinese friends arrived for breakfast, and by then, the coffee shop was filled with smoke. The tobacco companies were spreading their advertising dollars around Asia, and it seemed like everyone smoked everywhere.

We were on the road by 10:00 a.m., driving through small villages and the countryside. We saw some very poor areas with women carrying water from the town well. We drove up the Xigiao Mountain, to an area where people were letting off firecrackers, and there were stalls selling souvenirs. We were told that this was one of six sacred mountains in China. We bought some little fans for forty cents from an artist who would paint anything on them. We asked through Auntie if he would paint "Jesus loves you" on them. When he had finished, the crowd that had gathered thinned, and I was able to give him a copy of the Gospel of John in Chinese. He saw what it was, and I will always remember the delight on his face. He held his fist together and with the forward circling motion expressing Happy New Year to us. Then he gave me the thumbs-up sign that means "good" and said, *"shay, shay"* (thank you). I got goosebumps seeing his happiness in receiving God's Word. These are hungry people for the Word.

The ladies headed for the toilet area; I can still smell it. My Chinese friends took one look and said, "No, no." They wouldn't even go in it, so we waited until we got down the mountain and found a clean restroom. The area below seemed to be more popular, with many tour buses filled with Chinese. Auntie told me that most were from Hong Kong, and when asked how you can tell Hong Kong Chinese from Mainland Chinese, she said, "By their shoes."

We found a tourist-type restaurant that had poor service, and the food was awful. We were served chicken that was still bloody, a dish of black moss that looked like slime, and squid tentacles with snow peas and carrots. I ate the snow peas, carrots, and some rice. The soup was gray like dishwater. Shrimp with the heads on! I could still remember Christmas Eve when we were invited to dinner by several Chinese friends of Joel. They would grab the shrimp with their chopsticks and put the whole thing in their mouth. Then I could never figure out how they did it, but they would spit the shell out on the white tablecloth. By the time dinner was over, the table looked like a disaster area. Today's lunch was the same scenario.

Walking to the van, we stopped at a little cake shop and bought some special cakes that looked like pita bread but had a coarse cake texture, with a yeasty bread taste. This was a good substitute for lunch, together with some Mandarin oranges.

Oh, I would have loved a baked potato, but instead we had another banquet that evening. We were served a good-tasting chicken and watercress soup, but I didn't look in the bottom of the soup urn. We had pigeon, abalone, pigeon eggs with bamboo hearts and vegetables, Chinese ham and shrimp breaded in a fried flour dumpling, Shanghai bread (we love it), steamed bread, and a whole steamed tiger fish. Auntie got the head!

The next morning we left early, driving through more small towns and countryside villages. This trip gave us a marvelous opportunity to see the back roads of China and not just the sights that Western tourists get to see. We saw some pretty sad sights and people living in extreme hardships. We stopped in what was said to be a resort area and all got out to walk around instructing the van driver to meet us in another area.

The area was lovely, with a series of small bridges over a lake. There was a hotel in the midst of green hills, a Shangri-La with clouds low on the hills giving it a misty look. There was an old Chinese jet fighter plane on display. We walked tree-lined paths, on one side a type of palm tree and the other side had what looked like dead fir trees. We crossed the lake over a rocky obstacle course, jumping from one rocky step to the next until we got to a small island with concrete picnic tables. We walked down the road only to discover that we were probably not going in the right direction. We sent one of the children to find the van, realizing that the meet up details might not have been very accurate.

Our next destination was a very poor town with pigs walking in the streets. We turned down a dirt street, crossed a tiny bridge with no sides on it and parked near a canal. We were told this area was known for its ginger, straw (that is used to make rugs), and oranges. We were going to park and visit a paradise bird sanctuary. When we pulled up to park, a man came over with a pad in his hand collecting money for parking. There was a line of ladies sitting across the street selling dried orange peels. Chickens were running around, and the people other than the tourists were shabbily dressed.

The birds were large water birds, cranes that return to this area every evening and roost in the tall trees. We paid to go through the gate into the bird viewing area. There was a souvenir shop underneath and a couple of flights of stairs to look at the birds. A young girl came up to me and asked if she could practice her English. She was attending Guangzhou University and majoring in English. She spoke English very well, and I gave her an English/Chinese Gospel tract before we parted.

When we got back near the van, David decided to take some more pictures. We walked down the street, and there under a straw stack were two very large pigs sleeping. I urged David to be quiet and not wake the pigs, because I didn't want them chasing us. David spent most of his summers when he was growing up on his grandfather's farm in North Carolina. He told me not to be silly; pigs don't chase people. I could just imagine a couple of foreigners running down this dirt street being chased by large pigs. David walked over a very rickety wooden bridge about three feet wide and no sides. He got a picture of some ladies washing vegetables in the dirty canal water while other ladies a short distance away were washing their clothes. This was a very primitive setting, and I'm not sure the government would appreciate a couple of Westerners seeing all this.

In front of the van where we were parked was a small boat called a sampan that had been pulled up on the side of the shore. As we stood there, a little girl about ten years old came by, with no shoes and the seat of her pants in shreds. She got into the boat and my heart went out to her. Apparently this was where she lived. We decided to give her a "lucky" money packet with some Chinese money and a Gospel tract in it. We thought it best to wait until we were ready to leave so we would not attract a crowd and sent Joel to give it to her. This was southern China, which was supposed to be more prosperous. Can you imagine what other country sides might be like?

Along the drive, we passed bicycles carrying everything imaginable: three metal crates of pigs tied onto one bicycle, ducks in crates with their heads poking out, chickens with feathers flying in the breeze, and even a man who was delivering a wooden love seat and two chairs. Sometimes we'd see what appeared to be the mother, father, and child on one bicycle.

It was time for another lunch break, and this time in the city of Jian Men Shi at the Capital Hotel. We had lunch where the locals eat, and we all ate for a total of twenty-eight dollars. Quite often when a Westerner travels in China, the prices are inflated, but this trip with our Chinese friends, we were paying Chinese prices. It was a set lunch with roasted pork, a vegetable dish with mushrooms, chicken with black bean curd sauce and onions, sweet-and-sour pork, corn soup, squid with vegetables, fried bread, steamed bread, red bean dessert like a soup, fried rice, and noodles. The MSG (monosodium glutamate) was really getting to me. Besides the exhausted feeling that comes over me toward the end of each meal, I was now getting very flushed. My face got fire engine red and burned for a couple of hours after eating, all signs of an allergic reaction to MSG.

Throughout the trip, we had many opportunities to give out tracts and even some Bibles. Along the way back to Macau, Joel pointed out a church, and it was the first one we had seen the entire trip. We saw a hospital with a medical school attached, and Joel had the van stop while he ran into get Auntie a special tonic she takes called orange snake. The drive home was through a misty rain, and we saw a couple of accidents. I praised the Lord for His goodness and protection throughout this trip. It seemed like He reminded me of the "sow and reap" principle. As we rode in a van driven by Chinese, I remembered the many times David and I had driven vanloads of Chinese from Friends from Abroad to Hilton Head, Florida, North Carolina, and mountain parks. He has returned a hundredfold to us. We serve a mighty God and a generous Heavenly Father.

Back in Zhuhai, after what we had seen in other parts of Southern China, it looked so prosperous. We learned our driver had only met one other American in his life, and he had never seen anyone pray. Joel would always ask David to say the blessing at meals, and we had noted that the driver was always talking to Joel during the prayer. But the last lunch when David said, "Amen," I looked up and the driver still had his head bowed. When we said good-bye to our driver, we gave him a tip and a Gospel tract. We prayed for his salvation.

It was good to get back home to Macau, but it was a trip we will never forget, especially the man on the mountain who was so delighted to get a Gospel of John.

MORE CHINESE TREASURES

9

Before our return to Atlanta, we planned an extensive trip further into China. We did not want to take a tour and only see the tourist spots, but we wanted to experience the culture and the people of China. During our years working among international university students, we had become friends with several from China. They always expressed a desire for us to visit their homeland and their families who were still in China. We had invitations from families in Beijing and Shanghai.

We had heard that if we just showed up at a hotel in China and they saw our *"da beeza,"* the price would go up. We learned from a friend teaching English in China that Caucasian Westerners are often called "big noses" since the shape and size of the nose is different from the typical Chinese. So we worked with a travel agent in Hong Kong to book and pay in advance for our air and train tickets and hotel reservations. We were able to keep the costs down and stay in some five-star hotels. We would just have to show the prepaid vouchers. We were able to get a visa to visit China in Macau, which was about fifty percent cheaper than getting it in Hong Kong.

Our Chinese Auntie had invited us to stay in her Hong Kong apartment in order to fly out to Beijing the next morning. We met Auntie at the Macau Jetfoil early in the morning. She went to Hong Kong every Thursday to teach piano and had an ongoing first class reservation. We had an economy ticket and sat downstairs on the boat. After we were underway, she came down and gave us a box with a sugarcane drink that was given to her in first class.

It was a foggy morning, and there was a haze around Hong Kong when we arrived about an hour later. We followed Auntie, who knew the way through the terminal, immigration, and the subway system, to her apartment. The subway in Hong Kong was an excellent system and so very clean. We exited into the Kowloon side and came up to street level near the huge Muslim mosque. There was a large Muslim population in Hong Kong, and as we walked through the streets near the mosque, we saw Muslims from many countries of the world.

We walked a few blocks to her apartment (she owned five apartments in the building). At that time they were each selling for $1,500,000. The one she took us to was a tiny, cluttered, three-bedroom with a piano in one of the bedrooms. Auntie pointed out our room, which had two twin beds and enough room to stand when you shut the door (until we put our luggage in the room). The travel agency we had been working with was within walking distance from Auntie's apartment. Our tickets and vouchers were ready. We walked over to Singapore Airlines to confirm our return flight, an important detail unless you want to remain in China forever. We were avoiding China Air since we heard so many jokes about it. Some said the pilot left the cockpit to go to the toilet, and others said their seat fell through the floor.

After picking up some last-minute items, we visited the Christian Life Center, where we got some music cassettes in Mandarin to take with us. We bought Auntie a copy of *Streams in the Desert* in Chinese. Next door at New Life Ministries we were given tracts in simplified Chinese for our trip.

When we got back to Auntie's apartment, some of our other adopted family arrived. Joel's wife had arrived from Macau with a very bad sore throat and cold. She took some Chinese medicine and went to bed. Auntie also had a sore throat, and I prayed we would not take any of these germs to China. When Joel came, we went to the Windsor Hotel next door to meet Auntie's sister and her friend for lunch. On the way, we met a cousin of Auntie's on the street. He said he was Lisa's uncle. He had heard about our connection with Lisa in Atlanta.

Our lunch was very good Chinese and didn't seem to contain much MSG, which I had become allergic to. When we were ready to pay the bill, we were told that the uncle who hadn't even eaten with us had already taken care of it. We found that Chinese are very generous to their friends and gracious hosts/hostesses. Joel had arranged his stay in Hong Kong to take us sightseeing and make sure we got to the airport the next morning. Once again, he went out of his way to make sure we were safe. We have much to learn from Chinese friendship.

Joel had thoughtfully lit the water heater over the tub so that we could have a warm bath, which I enjoyed before climbing into bed. David decided to get up at 5:30 a.m. and take his. He woke up fast when the water was cold. Excited about an extended trip into China, we tiptoed to be very quiet and not wake everyone up. We were ready to leave and Joel popped out of his room. He insisted on taking us downstairs and putting us in a taxi. Off we went to the airport, checked in, went through immigration, security, and waited for the breakfast bar to open. I truly felt the Lord's presence, and I guess I needed a little reassurance. In the taxi, I had felt some pangs of fear and thought, "Imagine us going to Beijing all by ourselves; we must be crazy."

The plane was large, and we flew above the fog and clouds. We sat next to a Taiwanese salesman from Chicago who travels to China three out of four weeks each month. As the plane prepared to land in Beijing, we were told that the flight attendant would come by to collect all newspapers. We were not allowed to take foreign newspapers into China. We did find out later in the hotels that there were foreign newspapers and even CNN on the inter-hotel TV system. Our Chinese friends did not get the same news in their homes.

After we landed, I again had some feelings of fear. "I don't believe we are really here" was running through my mind. Then the Lord filled my mind with a song: "He Paid It All." I started humming and singing, "He did it all." As foreigners we stand out, so immediately we had an offer for a taxi at HK$200 (US$25), but when we got one later, it was US$6.20. The first taxi driver must have seen our "*da beeza.*"

We got our luggage and went through immigration and customs with no problems. We found our way upstairs to the Bank of China to exchange our money for FEC (foreign exchange currency). We went outside, where taxis were bringing people for departure and there was no competition to get one. There was a man getting out of a taxi, and he saw me and told the driver I was waiting. The Lord was providing every step of the way without speaking the language.

The taxi sped down the long Capital Airport Road. It was very cold, only 2–3° Celsius (35–37° Fahrenheit), and snow flurries were in the air. Snow-like fluffy white rice was on the cedar limbs that lined the road. The sky was gray and hazy like a portrait of Communist China: dark and dreary. That image continued as over the days we noticed that most people wore clothing that was dark and dreary.

We arrived at the four-star Landmark Hotel, which was only six months old, and there were two doormen to usher us into an empty lobby. We felt like we might be the only guests. Our voucher was for forty US dollars per night, different from the current price of $120. Our room was very nice, with the smell of new wood. We had been cautioned not to drink the water in China and noticed there was even a thermos of boiled water in the bathroom for brushing our teeth.

Our hotel was next door to the five-star Sheraton Great Wall, so we decided to have lunch over there. As we walked into the restaurant, we noticed a sign featuring a plain baked potato with choice of topping for 13.50 FEC. When we ordered it, the waitress didn't seem to understand us. She called the head waitress, who was just as puzzled by our request. I took her to the sign to show her what we wanted. We ended up with a plain baked potato, no topping and 7 FEC. We ordered water because we had heard all the water served is supposed to be boiled or bottled. The water had small black specks floating on top, so we decided to order bottled water. The water arrived and was mineral water and tasted like Alka-Seltzer. Lunch cost a total of seven US dollars and half that was for water. We stopped at the hotel restroom, and the attendant doted over me. She turned on the water, pushed the soap dispenser, handed me a towel, and there was a brush; if I needed brushing she would do it. We checked on day tours and there was one to the Great Wall and Ming Tombs for 130 FEC or US$26 each.

One of the Chinese students we had met at Georgia Tech had insisted we contact his mother, Mei, while we were in Beijing. When we got back to our hotel, we tried to call her, but learned she was away and would not return until we had left Beijing. Her daughter spoke a little English and asked our name and phone number. Mei was one of the "two Chinese grandmothers" I had taken on a tour to the Governor's Mansion back in the States. Neither spoke English, so we had a day of sign language and lots of smiles. She also went with us and about twenty-five other Chinese on a trip we organized to David's cousin's farm in North Carolina.

We wanted to contact our friend Wen, who we met at Friends from Abroad. We had spent many hours with Wen, who loved music and even took one of First Baptist Atlanta's hymnals back to China. We got to know her quite well after she came along with us when we drove a couple of vans full of Chinese to Hilton Head for Thanksgiving. A church sponsored the trip and hosted the internationals in members' homes.

I only had her address, so I enlisted the assistance of the lady at the guest relations services desk. Miss Wang made several calls to inquire about Wen's phone number. We silently prayed, but it looked like a dead end. We had built a friendship with Wen and hoped to renew it here in China.

I was called to the front desk for a phone call. It was a call from a translator at Mei's home. I glanced back to Miss Wang's desk, and David was on the phone with Wen. Praise the Lord, the contacts were made. Mei's family wanted us to come for dinner on Saturday evening and they would come to the hotel and take us to their apartment. I went over to Miss Wang's desk and was able to talk with Wen. We arranged for her to come Sunday morning and asked her to spend the day and go to the Great Wall with us. We invited her husband and two sons to join us also. She would call back the next morning and let us know.

We took a taxi to the Temple of Heaven's east gate. We paid the small entrance fee and walked through the snow-lined paths. It was fun to see young people having snowball fights and building snowmen. The Temple of Heaven was so interesting. We had been in a replica of it at Epcot, but the real one was much larger. Inside was an altar with four surrounding altars, each holding a calf made of stone. These were symbolic of the sacrifices that used to take place here. This is actually the place the emperor came to ask heaven for a good harvest. It was a display of idol worship taking place during the Qing and Ming dynasties.

We found a toilet using our "Where is the toilet?" card. This card was nearly worn to shreds by the time we left China. As I approached the toilet, which consisted of a hole in the floor with an indented footmark on each side, I had to laugh. It was cold and I was bundled up with layers of clothing and was about to squat down so that I would not splash all over me. First I had to get the slacks and long underwear down. Then the jacket and sweater needed to be pulled up, and what about the long scarf that dangled in front, just missing the hole in the floor? A great exercise in culture adjustment!

We spent the rest of the day walking through the large grounds, past some other ancient buildings, and out the south gate. We prayed for a taxi as well as another toilet. As we walked along the street we tried to hail a couple of taxis with no success. It was beginning to get dark and cooler, and David was getting desperate for a toilet. He started looking down isolated alleys for relief, since there was only one McDonald's in Beijing. He tried a small food store, or maybe it was a bakery, to no avail. Our prayers were getting more fervent as we rounded a corner. He saw a man open a door, and David ran up ahead and flashed his toilet card. The man motioned upstairs, and when he got to the top of the stairs, a lady directed him to a toilet and even turned on the light when she saw "the card." Praise the Lord for His provisions throughout China.

David came down the stairs looking more comfortable and pulled another card out of his pocket. He flashed the "We want a taxi, please" card at the same man at the door. He motioned for us to follow him outside, where he became involved in a conversation with another man and a woman. We interpreted their sign language to mean under the bridge in front of us and around to the left. As we crossed the street toward the bridge, a taxi came along and stopped when David flagged it. Oh, good! The lady driver took a look at our Landmark Hotel card, shook her head, and motioned in the same direction as the others. Off we went, under the bridge, across the street, and to the left, all the time dodging bicycles. No taxi in sight and now it was getting dark in a strange place. We hoped the Lord had heard our call for a taxi. We spotted another taxi; before we could get there, it moved on.

We could see a restaurant just ahead of us and considered stopping in to ask about a taxi. Before we went in, we stood at the curb and up pulled a taxi dropping a man off. We decided to get in and then show the hotel's card. Maybe we would have squatter's rights. He took off and it made some awful noises. Laughing, David said, "He has a problem: the engine is missing." The driver realized he had a problem when it came to a halt in the middle of a long bridge. Getting out he opened the hood and tinkered as we prayed. Actually that gave me time to deposit a Chinese tract in the tray between the front seats. The driver got it started, and off we went to the hotel.

After shedding our long underwear, we had dinner in the hotel's Chinese restaurant. Hot and sour soup warms all of you at once. Shanghai fried bread, pork with sweet-and-sour sauce, fried noodles with shredded pork, and Chinese petit fours (dough shaped like cute tiny chickens filled with red bean paste) completed the meal. After a day of lots of walking in the brisk air, we had a wonderful night's sleep. Pulling the curtains open in the morning, I saw the American flag flying along with the Chinese flag at the Sheraton across the street. Wen called and would come to meet us the next day at 9:00 a.m., so the three of us could go to the Great Wall.

We had an American breakfast in the hotel's Western restaurant. We had been warned by our Hong Kong travel agent to make sure that as soon as we arrive in a new city to confirm our air tickets. She said if we did not, they may cancel our reservations. The hotel guest relations lady confirmed them and ordered the car and driver for the next day to the Great Wall.

It was easy to get a taxi at the hotel, so off we went to Tiananmen Square. We decided to get out at the far end and walk through the Square so we could take some pictures. We noticed people looking at us and then realized we were the only Westerners in sight. We found steps to a tunnel under the street and crossed to the Palace Museum also known as the Forbidden City. As we walked through the south gate, we saw a sign for foreigners to go to the right and Chinese to the left. All through our travels in China we learned that there were two prices; foreigners usually pay two or three times the Chinese price. There was only one foreign man in front of us and the rest of the crowd went to the left. Through the day, we observed that many people from the countryside were visiting Beijing. Many were poorly dressed and some had on the blue Mao suits. We also concluded that most had not seen many Westerners, if any, because they would just stand and stare at us or go by us and turn back and look.

We paid the entrance fee (US$3.60 each) and rented one of the tape recorders with an English tour (US$4.40). It was an interesting three and a half hours as we learned about the Qing and Ming dynasties. Perhaps this would give us a better understanding of our Chinese friends' culture. It was very cold, and the marble and cement paths added to the chill. Even though it was cold, I enjoyed every minute of exploring the historical buildings and learning about the emperors' lifestyles. The wealth that existed among the emperors was staggering. They even collected the hairs that fell from the empress' head and kept them in a porcelain jar. I thought about what the Bible says, "But even the hairs of your head are all numbered" (Matt. 10:30).

I saw my first split pants on a baby. As I understood, babies don't wear diapers in China, but these split pants enable the mother to squat the baby to do their business. It could be in the gutter or anywhere they desire. We found a pay toilet, and upon entering we were given a couple of sheets of pink toilet paper. There was a bar of soap (one for the four sinks) tied to one of the sinks with a piece of string through a hole in the center.

We left the Forbidden City through the north gate and walked along the street, looking for Bei Hai Park (North Sea Park). We found the entrance and paid the twenty cents to get in. It was getting late in the day and colder. The map had showed a teahouse, and we thought we could warm up a bit there. It didn't open for another twenty minutes, but as we walked on, we found Ruby's Bakery, where we had hot tea and a piece of cake. It was an oasis. We walked around the other side and out to the street to find a taxi. This time it was a tiny van (a miniature Volkswagen) and we got back to the hotel for only two US dollars.

We went up to our room to freshen up, and around 6:30 p.m. we got a call that SB, the translator for Mei's son-in-law, Jian, was downstairs waiting for us. Again, we found that Chinese go above and beyond to take care of their friends. They had arranged for the translator, the use of a car, and a friend of theirs was the driver for the evening. We rode across Beijing to Mei's apartment and through the gates and pulled up in the back of the building right next to the door that led upstairs to the apartment. The place she worked provided her housing. We climbed the four flights of cement stairs to the apartment and met her daughter, Yuling, who had been born there and has lived there for thirty-five years. The eleven-year-old grandson was so thrilled to have us visit. Mei was away visiting another son in another province, but the rest of the family turned out to entertain us. She had told her family to make sure to care for us. The living room had a TV, sofa, two soft chairs, and a small round table where we had dinner. We had a superb dinner with about twenty dishes prepared by Yuling. They were a gracious and hospitable family. All evening, we talked through the translator, and they seemed to enjoy hearing about Atlanta. We talked about how we had met Mei while she was visiting her son, who was working on his doctorate at Georgia Tech. They had heard about the international friendship group we directed. Mei had told them that after the weekly luncheon she went to the optional class to learn English. Suddenly the grandson jumped up and came running back into the living room with a Bible. It was the Bible we had given Mei. Chills went through me as I realized that the Bible had made it back to Beijing, and everyone seemed to know where it was kept.

We had brought some gifts: a pair of panty hose for Mei, a pretty hand towel, another Chinese Bible, and a cassette tape of Christian music sung by Christians in China. They gave us a key chain with the Great Wall and Asian games on it and a wall hanging in bamboo. When they drove us back to the hotel, they asked several times if there was anything they could do for us while we were in Beijing. We had been kind to their family in the USA and they wanted to make sure we were taken care of in China.

The next morning, we were up early and excited because Wen was going with us to the Great Wall. We had hardly finished another good American breakfast when we got a call that Wen was downstairs. We asked her to come up to our room and we ran to the elevator to meet her. It had been two years since she left Atlanta, and we had a lot of catching up to do. Her husband wasn't able to join us, but we would meet him for dinner. He had also studied in Atlanta several years before she did. He was befriended by a Christian while in Atlanta and was taken on a mission trip to Kansas to help build a church. When he returned to Beijing, he took his family to a church. When asked if he was a Christian, he replied that he wasn't, and they said he could not come in.

Wen suggested we go to the Great Wall at Mutianyu rather than Badaling, which was quite commercialized. The desk called to say that our van was waiting. David sat in front with the driver, while Wen and I shared the second seat in the tiny van. Wen told the driver where we wanted to go, and we headed across Beijing. The further we went, the more I began to question the direction, since the Great Wall we wanted to go to was northeast, and we were headed northwest. We finally got it across to the driver, through Wen, where we wanted to go. Communication even when someone speaks the same language can be difficult. The driver didn't have a map and had to stop and ask directions several times. He took us though a lot of countryside north of Beijing, which we would not have seen if he had gone the right way in the first place. We saw sheep crossing the road, mules pulling wagons, and many new and different sights. We drove along a canal with the road lined on each side with tall, barren trees. We crossed a bridge with a pretty stream flowing and small mountains surrounded us. We learned from Wen that the driver was not of the majority Han but was Man (Manchu) or Ma ethic minority.

When we reached Mutianyu, we walked up the hill past the hawkers and booths selling everything from postcards, and T-shirts to quilts, and fur hats. Wen negotiated for a black fur hat for David and T-shirts for gifts. The entrance tickets were the same price for foreigners and Chinese, but the cable car was three times more for the foreigners even though we rode in the same car. As we walked up the hill, we came across a man offering rides on his two camels. He wanted to know if we wanted a ride or just sit on them and take pictures. Mules were also standing by to be offered to the foreigners. We chose to take the cable car, and it was a magnificent view as we rode to the top.

We could see the Great Wall outlined on the ridge at the top and the beautiful valley below. The Wall was covered with snow, and I think we took one hundred pictures. There were very few people at this part of the Great Wall, whereas at Badaling we had heard sometimes there were so many tourists you couldn't get a shot of just the Wall. We walked down along the wall, the dirt path, and stairs. Our knees hurt toward the bottom and we felt those muscles for days to come. What a day! It took two hours to get to the Wall and only one hour to get back. Our only stop on the way back was to see where they held the Asian games.

We drove to the area near Wen's apartment, and she went to get her family. As we waited, we noticed many people on bicycles going in a nearby driveway and each carrying several thermos bottles. We learned this was the boiler house, where people came to get their boiled water. It was a different way of life in China in the 90s.

Our driver waited and drove us, along with Wen and her husband and two teenage sons to a small Muslim restaurant near Bei Hai Park. We were the only foreigners in the restaurant. They specialized in barbecued lamb and Peking duck. It was very reasonable and delicious. During dinner, Wen told us that she wanted her sons to go to college in the United States.

Wen needed to be home by 8:00 p.m. in order to get their milk. Milk is allotted only to children and old people. Aren't we spoiled? By the time we finished eating, the restaurant was empty. People seem to head home early, since most streets do not have lights. The taxi got us back in time for the milk, and we sadly said good-bye to our friends. We agreed to meet Wen the next day to go to the Summer Palace together.

Two days with Wen was wonderful, and we spent a lot of the time talking about God. She told us she had the Bible she had received in Atlanta and had hopes her sons would become Christians. We had a couple of Bibles with us and asked her if she knew someone who would like them. After her gracious Chinese, "You might need them," she took them for her friends.

We took a taxi back to our hotel, praising the Lord all the way for a special day with a special friend. We had tried not to drink during the trip to the Great Wall because good restrooms were very scarce, so we downed lots of water before going to bed. We did not rush out in the morning but waited for Wen's call. She called to say she got the afternoon off and wanted us to meet her for lunch before going to the Summer Palace.

Wen had given us directions on where to meet her, and the hotel concierge relayed the directions for the taxi driver. We only waited about ten minutes before Wen rode up on her bicycle. She said we would eat at the special foreign guest dining hall, where she had made reservations. I'm sure she spent a lot of money to treat us to lunch. We saw tables with foreign students as we walked through to a small room. One table seemed to be occupied by an American group, and a man greeted us with "hello" when we walked past.

We washed up at a sink in the corner with soap and three community towels hanging. We had another banquet with sweet-and-sour fish, tiny whole birds with head and legs on, beef marrow with mushrooms, rice, scallops with an unknown sea morsel, fried chicken, shrimp, and orange pop to drink. After lunch, she took the leftovers home and returned, leaving her bicycle to pick up later. We had told Wen we wanted to ride a local bus with her because we were afraid to venture out on one alone. The buses are usually packed, and then someone standing outside the bus shoves a few more on.

When we got on the bus with Wen, it was not too crowded, and she paid the fare. There were ladies in booths in the middle and rear of the bus who sold tickets. David spotted two buckets on the floor and asked Wen about them. They were to get water in case the bus got overheated. The bus coughed, the gears ground, and sometimes it stalled. We were fortunate to get seats as people got off, because the Summer Palace was at the end of the line.

The Summer Palace was built by an emperor who liked to visit Suzhou but didn't want to travel so far. We were blessed today to have our own private tour guide and friend explaining that Suzhou Street was a reproduction of Suzhou in the south of China. We climbed a multitude of steps to the highest point, and at the top there was a tower filled with Buddhist statues. One of the buildings had small Buddhists carved into the exterior with all their heads missing. Wen explained that during the Cultural Revolution, many historical sites were destroyed, and we witnessed signs of that throughout the day. Other than Suzhou Street, the Summer Palace did not seem very interesting, and everything looked run-down. Our upper thighs and the backs of our calves were sore from the steps at the Great Wall. Maybe we were getting tired. We found a place to sit by Kumming Lake that was made to look like the Xiwu Lake in Hangzhou (soon to be another city we would visit). We rested and talked and had probably some of our most precious moments with our friend. We opted for a taxi instead of the local bus and dropped Wen off to pick up her bike. I felt sad saying good-bye. It had been so good to be with our *pengyou* (friend) again.

SHANGHAI FRIENDS

10

The next morning, we flew on to Shanghai on a modern Boeing 767 on China Airlines. Shanghai immediately appeared different than Beijing. The taxi dispatching was very orderly with a man in charge who spoke English. We soon observed that everyone wanted to practice his or her English, from the taxi driver to the doorman at the hotel. Our hotel was a high-rise glass tower near the old Jin Jiang Hotel. We had purchased vouchers, so we knew the price would not go up when they saw us.

After getting settled in our room, we went for a walk along Nanking Road and stopped in at the famous Nanking Road No. 1 Department Store. We bought some enamel bracelets and a set of decorative chopsticks for gifts. We noticed a cross on top of a church in the distance. We stopped in at the old Peace Hotel with its marble walls and floors. It must have been a show place when it was built in 1929 and originally named The Cathay. I heard the hotel once hosted Charlie Chaplin, George Bernard Shaw and Noel Coward. The Cathay's tea dances sold out months in advance, and Sir Victor Sassoon, the hotel's Iraqi-Jewish owner, lived in the green, copper pyramid on the roof. The hotel was later taken over by the Communist government and it gradually lost the luster that had once made it the most famous hotel in Asia.

We walked along until we reached the waterfront that is called the Bund, where for years Chinese students would practice English. We looked out at the busy harbor, and as we were standing there, we were approached by three young men. We were overwhelmed by the boldness here in Shanghai compared with just stares in Beijing. I was immediately suspect of these young men's motives. We talked for a few minutes and then moved on, only to be approached by one of the same men again. Later, some Chinese friends said that there are some strange people hanging out at the Bund, including some spies, and many scams take place around there. We decided to get away from the area and walked two blocks to check out a restaurant that was listed in a travel book as an old German Restaurant. It was full of smoke and it was a dark, dingy place, so we could hardly get out of there fast enough.

We were weary from our travel and decided we would walk back to the hotel, have dinner, and just relax. After dinner, we learned that we had two messages from Cheng's family. Cheng Wong was a doctorate student at an Atlanta university and came to Friends from Abroad on a regular basis. We had shared many good times together. He had been over to our house for dinner several times, and he had joined in the holiday trips sponsored by Friends from Abroad. When he learned we were going to Macau, he told us he had written to his parents in China, and they were expecting us to come to visit. We returned their message, and they were disappointed we could not come to dinner that evening. It really worked out for the best, because I was feeling overloaded, yucky, and maybe a cold coming with sore muscles. I was in bed by 7:30.

After a good night's sleep and breakfast, I was still not feeling real good, so I took one of those large white pills to stop diarrhea and it did the trick. Mary (her English name), Cheng's girlfriend, had told us last night on the phone that she would pick us up at the hotel at 10:00 a.m. We had a full day ahead, with sightseeing followed by dinner at Cheng's parents' apartment. Again, we were to learn what lengths Chinese will go to entertain friends. When the car pulled up, Mary was accompanied by Cheng's older sister, Huan. Another sister, Li, had a friend with a taxi company and arranged for the use of a taxi with a driver for the day. I was so impressed with their generosity. At that time, these dear Chinese friends were not allowed to come into the hotel. In fact, when we returned to the hotel that evening, they stood outside the windows and waved to us when we went into the lobby. So humbling!

Mary spoke English very well and was our interpreter, because Huan and the rest of the Wong family only spoke Chinese. I felt an immediate love for these girls. Huan was a tall, large-boned girl, and I remarked that our facial features were similar. She was thirty-six, married, and had a four year old son.

They drove us to Old Shanghai, and we walked through the narrow, crowded streets. There were a lot of foreign tourists there, but we also saw Chinese who looked like they were from the countryside. We walked through the old village, admiring the unique buildings, and wandering into shops with interesting things to buy, but most of all looking at the people. We crossed the zigzag bridge, and the girls explained that it was designed to confound evil spirits that can only walk in straight lines. Interesting! We walked past the old teahouse where Queen Elizabeth is said to have had tea. We took pictures as we walked through the Yu Yuan Garden (means Garden of Happiness) that was built in 1559. It had originally been a private garden of the Ming dynasty and is a famous Chinese classical garden. The garden had interesting Chinese architecture with artwork on the buildings. Some of the walls were stone carved, depicting an ancient story. Others had long dragons forming the edge of the roof. There were ponds and stone bridges throughout. What a treat walking through history and talking with these sweet Chinese ladies.

Mary told me that she had tried to get to the United States by asking the Georgia State Representative to write a letter to the Shanghai Consulate. It didn't do any good, but she continued to try. All her requests for a visa were denied because they felt that she would not return to China. I sensed Mary seemed very open to learning about Jesus. I believe she had been told by Cheng that David and I were Christians.

We stopped to have some dumplings, sometimes called pot stickers, yummy small pockets of dough filled with vegetables or meat or seafood that are steamed, fried, and dipped in a sauce. All the tables were full, and I mentioned to the girls that I was having a little problem with my stomach and thought I would wait until dinner to eat. They decided they would buy a variety of rolls, cakes, and sandwiches that could be eaten in the taxi as we rode through Shanghai.

Our taxi was waiting for us, and as we drove off, Mary asked me if a Christian could go in a Buddhist temple. We said we could, and she explained that she wanted to show us the Jade Buddha. The question had opened up some interesting conversation about the difference between Buddhism and Christianity. Upon entering the temple, we soon realized that it was not a tourist site but a functioning Buddhist temple. This was a perfect spot to explain more about the differences in Christianity and Buddhism. We saw people entering, bowing, and praying to the Buddha. We passed several huge golden Buddha that lined the side of the temple, some with frightening, grotesque faces. People were buying joss sticks (incense) to burn at the altar and waving some of the burning sticks in front of the Jade Buddha. Mary said that the young people of China are searching for something to believe in. This temple tour was such an answer to prayer. We would be able to share Jesus and the Bible's teachings with our friends. We mentioned that we would like to see a Christian church. Mary told us she went to one with a friend quite often and said she would take us by it today. Mary asked us if the US government owns the churches.

As we continued along the streets of Shanghai, Mary told me a story about meeting an older lady in the park one day who had a younger girl with her. Both of them spoke English, and Mary liked to practice her English, so she sat for a long time talking with them. They talked about the Bible and Jesus. The lady asked if she would like to come to her hotel to talk more privately, and Mary felt she could trust her, so she went along. One of Mary's Chinese friends was with her and went too. When the Chinese go to a hotel to visit a foreigner, I learned they must sign in. They both signed their name, and the friend listed her address as requested. They spent some time talking about the Bible and then left. A few days later, the other Chinese girl got a visit from someone in the government who questioned her about her visit to the foreigner's room. He asked her many questions, including if the lady had given her any literature. He told her she should never see that lady again. I had thought that Chinese were not allowed in the foreigner's hotel, but the concern is that if they go in, they must sign in and therefore are in fear of a visit from a government official.

We drove across the city and pulled up in front of a huge, old Neo-Gothic Roman Catholic Cathedral. The iron gate was locked, but a man came out, and the driver said something to him in Chinese, and he opened the gate for us to drive thru. We pulled right up in front of the steps and walked in the main door, pulling aside the heavy hanging drape that kept the cold out or in. It felt colder inside than outside. It was a beautiful old cathedral, with high ceilings adorned with statues, carvings, and paintings. There were many different alcoves and some were where the confessional booths were located.

Research about this very old cathedral uncovered that in 1955 the bishop had been arrested and sentenced to life imprisonment. In 1966, at the start of the Cultural Revolution, the Red Guards from Beijing vandalized the cathedral, tearing down its spires and smashing the stained glass, and spent three days burning most of the Catholic books. Red Guards beat up priests and nuns. A church leader knelt at the altar and prayed until he was dragged away for the duration of the Cultural Revolution. He was sent for labor training repairing umbrellas and washing bottles. For the next ten years, the Cathedral had served as a state owned grain warehouse. In 1978, the cathedral was reopened, and the spires were restored in the early 1980s. In 1989, the first Chinese language Mass was celebrated. Imagine that was only about a year before I stood in the cathedral with my Chinese friends listening to a group of about ten old ladies praying at the altar. Mary and I had just visited a Buddhist temple where ladies were praying, and now here in this old cathedral were other ladies praying. Mary began to ask questions about prayer. I told Mary we pray directly to God and there is only one mediator, Jesus. The Bibles states in 1 Timothy 2:5, "For there is one God and there is one mediator between God and men, the man Christ Jesus."

We noticed that the taxi driver had become curious and was looking through the plastic window in the door drape. David invited him to come in, and we learned that it was his first time in a church. I had a little booklet, "How to Know God," in Chinese and English. I looked up scripture about Jesus as the only mediator and showed Mary. She translated that scripture and other scriptures. What an opportunity to share about Jesus! I was reminded how Jesus shared with people as He walked along. I could not have orchestrated this evangelistic moment. It had to be the Holy Spirit working through me. What an exciting day in China and it was going to continue for several more hours! I asked Mary if I could give the driver a Bible, and she asked him if he would like one. He told her he would.

Next stop was the train station to exchange vouchers for tickets for our trip to Hangzhou the next day. The plaza in front of the train station was filled with peasants from the countryside waiting for trains. I didn't experience much fear when in China, except when I was near a crowd of peasants. Living in the countryside, they usually had not seen a Westerner, and probably they were afraid of us too. I was thankful to have Mary with us to get us to the soft seat waiting room. The waiting room was plush by Chinese standards and filled with sofas and potted plants. David and Mary stood in line to exchange the vouchers, only to learn that they were really the tickets and we could use them tomorrow. It was good that we came, because we learned where the station was and all the details about our trip. We saw that the train listings were both in English and Chinese. Mary wrote a card for us to give to the taxi driver saying to take us to the train station. I felt confident that we could find our way the next day.

As we drove along toward Cheng's parents' apartment for dinner, we saw men working on a sidewalk along a wall. Mary told us that the building across the street was going to be worked on, and the people living there would be moved out to temporary housing. The temporary housing would extend from the wall onto the sidewalk. I had read about this type of temporary housing in "Life and Death in Shanghai." Nien Chang wrote her autobiography while in exile in the United States. It was about her six-year imprisonment during the Cultural Revolution. She was arrested in 1966, after the Red Guards looted her home. Her late husband worked for a major American oil company in Shanghai. She refused to provide a false confession and was tortured. She was released in 1973 and learned her daughter had been murdered. She was not allowed to return to her spacious home but was relocated to a small apartment. She was under constant surveillance for years. Finally, in 1980, when the political climate improved, she was able to get a visa to the United States to visit family and never returned. This had been an eye-opening trip for me, and my heart goes out to those who have suffered so much while we in the United States have experienced freedom and abundance.

In this Communist country, people were generally provided housing from their employer in stark-looking concrete buildings with several floors. We were about to enter our first and experience the warmth of Chinese hospitality. The hallway was very dark and the elevator had a light bulb dangling down. When the elevator stopped on the ninth floor, it was about a foot below the floor, so we had to step up in order to get out. The apartment consisted of one room that served as the living room, dining room, and bedroom combined. A tiny kitchen and bathroom completed the small apartment. We were told that there was another small room that was formerly Cheng's. The Wong's had lived in this apartment for years and raised their three children here. The floors were cement, and there did not appear to be any heat in the apartment. We learned later that from Shanghai south that heat was not provided in government buildings. We all sat with our coats on through dinner and the evening. The apartment was clean and very neat.

We were warmly greeted by Mr. and Mrs. Wong. She reminded me of my Aunt Grace who had a sweet, gentle face. We were asked to sit at a small table and served tea and sweet dumplings filled with sesame seeds. Mary sat with us to translate while dinner was being prepared. After tea, we were moved over to a large table where others sitting on the bed and the sofa could join us for dinner. We ate for three hours as we were served the biggest banquet of Chinese food we had ever seen. I counted twenty different dishes, and we were expected to eat from each one. David did his usual good job of eating and made everyone feel good. I nibbled here and there. Li, the younger daughter, did a lot of the cooking, so her mother was able to sit at the table with us. It was so humbling, because we knew that it must have taken most of their month's income to splurge on us. Most Chinese families cannot afford to purchase a whole chicken.

Before we finished eating, an uncle of Cheng's came in. He told us his daughter was in Detroit, studying computer at a university. We were humbled more as they presented us with gifts: a wool sweater for David, a set of small porcelain vases for me, along with two hand-painted fans, and four boxes of Jasmine tea. We had brought some small gifts for Mrs. Wong: a hand towel, a pair of pantyhose, and a Bible. They were wrapped when we handed them to her, and as the custom, she put them aside for later. Chinese do not usually open gifts in front of the giver.

Mr. Wong brought out a photo album that Cheng had sent from Atlanta. David pointed out that he was in one of pictures with Cheng. There were other pictures of American Christians who had befriended Cheng on some of the Friends from Abroad trips and in home socials. It was an evening of laughter, smiles, picture taking, with Mary translating. Each daughter had a son, then ages four and five. They were a little frightened of us at first because we were the first foreigners they had seen. We fell in love with the family. We gave both sisters and Mary a Bible in Chinese. We gave Mary a cassette tape of Christian hymns sung by Christians in China in Mandarin. I pray that they will come to know Jesus as their Savior and I will see them in heaven someday.

When it came time to leave, they had arranged for a van to take us back to the hotel. The whole family piled into the van. When we got to the hotel, we all got out on the sidewalk to say our good-byes. When we went inside, they were looking in the window waving. They did not dare venture in the hotel and have to sign in for fear of a visit from a government official. What a blessing the day had been!

The next morning, we went up to the observation tower on the fortieth floor to take some pictures of Shanghai. It was a cold and windy morning as we took a taxi to the train station and waited in the soft seat waiting room until our train was called. I walked through the room looking at the potted plants and noticed a room marked "boiled water." I guess that is where people fill their thermos. We sure take things for granted in the United States.

NEW EXPERIENCES

11

The train to Hangzhou was listed on a board announcing departures in Chinese and English. We didn't have any problems. I think the travel agencies try to scare Americans about travel in China so they can sell tours. We took the tall escalator up, and when we neared Track 2 and 3, there was a rush of people crossing our path. These were Chinese who were coming through another gate and probably running to get a seat on the train. We were going to the soft seat car where our seats were reserved, costing six US dollars each. The Chinese could not afford to travel that way and were herded into cars on the train, where the first there got the seats and the rest stood without room to even sit on the floor.

A lady in a blue uniform was standing at our car, and we saw her later on the train. I guess she was our conductor or attendant. We boarded the train and our seats were close by. They were covered with a red slipcover and protected by a white lace doily. There was a small table in front of our seat with a white cloth and enamel tray on it. Attendants came by with boiling water after we were on our way. The Chinese sitting across from us had their tea leaves in a glass jar with screw lids, which seemed like a very practical item to carry with you on a train.

Soon after boarding, to our disappointment, a tour of Americans boarded. They were noisy and I think culturally insensitive. We were thankful that their seats were at the other end of the car. We were soon underway, passing fields of green vegetables. I felt like I had moved back in time. It was a slow-moving train with frequent stops. I was thankful for the sign in Chinese that graphically showed "no smoking or spitting" on the train. Everyone seems to smoke in China. I felt like I had spent days in a smokehouse. My throat was sore and my chest hurt.

An attendant sat down on the seat in front of us, across the little table from me. She was doing paperwork. She was probably in her early twenties, and when she finished her work, I spoke to her in my limited Chinese, and soon we were having English lessons. She got up and said "bye-bye." I sat looking out the window, rethinking some of my experiences in Beijing and Shanghai. One of the things that impressed me in Beijing, and probably it is true throughout China, was the lunch schedules. Wen and her husband got two hours for lunch and their children got the same two hours. They all met at home for lunch and a time for discussion. Wen believes this time helps them keep the communication open with their sons. I think it is a great idea too. Years ago, the American family would come home for lunch, but now it is rare for a family to even have dinner together.

Well, it came time to check out the toilet that was at the other end of the car. It was fairly clean at the beginning of the trip, but as time went by it got dirtier, and toward the end of the trip I had to hold my breath while in it. It was a typical hole-in-the-floor toilet. We noticed a policeman walking through the car every so often. He came by once and sat down in the seat in front of me. I said, "Ni hao," and tried my other limited Chinese on him. He liked it and got interested. He got up and came back with a sheet of paper, and I could tell he wanted English lessons. We had a good time, and soon the attendant and another railroad worker came to listen. We now had a class of three. We took their pictures before the train stopped at Hangzhou. David had a long conversation with a young man in his early thirties from Shanghai who worked for the railroad administration and was travelling free for a holiday in Hangzhou.

When we left the train, the two ladies helped me off and the policeman pointed us in the direction for a taxi. We went up the stairs and ran into throngs of Chinese who were running along from the other cars. We spotted the soft seat waiting room and asked the girl at the door about a taxi. She pointed us through the waiting room and out the other side. It was dark now, and the area had poor lighting. A fence went all around the station, and we could not find a gate to get out. The darkness and the crowds were a little intimidating for me. We walked back and forth in front of the station searching for a gate.

We breathed a prayer to the Lord for a taxi, and about that time we saw a group of men who looked like they might be taxi drivers on the other side of the fence. They looked eager to take a foreigner. We said "taxi" and then hand-motioned, asking how we could get out of there. They pointed to a gate, and two ladies opened it and let us out. We soon learned that they were indeed eager to take a foreigner when they started asking for fifty yuan. We said, *"Tai quay,"* which means "too expensive," and continued to walk. The prices offered ranged from twenty-five to fifty, and then we found a driver who would take us for twenty. We learned later that the price should have been fourteen. It was dark, a strange town; we were lost and had no choice but to pay more. Even then, the driver would not use his meter. We drove through the dark city and past Xiwu Lake (West Lake) to a large hotel that was part of the Shangri-La chain joint venture. We checked in and had dinner in a Western restaurant. We needed a good night's sleep.

We were up early on Friday, March 15, and it was raining. The restaurant served a Western breakfast, and David got his eggs cooked to order by a chef from Indiana. We planned to fly from Hangzhou to Guilin and had to confirm our air reservations. The hotel service desk was happy to assist us for a US$4 fee. We took a walk to China Travel to learn more about Hangzhou and tours available. We got a map and decided to walk around the area and prayed the rain would let up. Just in case we got lost, we made a note on the map of our hotel location, which faced the large lake.

We crossed the street and walked over the bridge which led to an island. We stopped to buy an umbrella with Xiwu Lake scenes on it. We crossed the bridge at the other end of the island and walked along a main street, looking for the Hangzhou Silk Factory. We found a side street that looked like the right direction, and sure enough, it ended up in front of the factory gate. We met a young man who spoke some English, and he told us it was lunchtime and to come back later for a factory tour.

We had some time to kill, so decided we would try to find the Friendship Store where foreigners could shop. Instead, we ended up walking past the bus station, where crowds of peasants from the countryside were waiting. Here again I felt a little intimidated, or maybe downright scared when we were approached by some Tibetan-looking people who had bags of jaws and horns from yaks or reindeer. They were pushing them in front of our faces, wanting us to buy these special medical cures. They also had large balls of fur about the size of baseballs for sale, along with daggers. I never did figure out what the fur was for…maybe knitting?

We quickly crossed the street and saw a large store that turned out to be a local department store. By this time I was in need of a bathroom, and David got out his "Where is the toilet?" card. We were directed to a side hallway, where we met a girl just unlocking what looked like a switchboard room. She showed us where the toilets were located. When we came back, we stopped to ask her where the Friendship Store was on our map. She also wrote down its Chinese name. She spoke some English, and we thanked her for her help and gave her a copy of "How to Know God." I felt like the Lord had led us to this girl, one of his divine appointments. Throughout our trip in China, we continued to see His hand moving us in directions where we had divine encounters with people. Praise Him!

Since we were in the store, we looked around and found a counter that sold tea. Hangzhou is noted for its Dragon Well tea. We bought three packages and some pretty lace valance material sold by the meter and very reasonably priced. We thought it would look good in our apartment when we got back to Atlanta and would remind us of our China trip. Whenever we stopped to look at something in a store, we soon attracted a crowd who would watch us. We were on our own in China and not with a tour, so we were off the beaten path among the people. Most of the store doors had heavy drapes over them instead of doors. Once David was going out and another man was coming in; they collided.

We finally found the Friendship Store, but it was tiny and didn't have much merchandise. I talked with a lady at the counter, and before I left I gave her a tract. Walking back to the silk factory, we saw more peasants selling their wares. Some of the young men were wearing a metal block hanging around their neck. I didn't understand what it was about. Along the way, people approached us wanting to exchange our money. Also, during the day, David was approached by two men trying to sell him a large coin.

When we got back to the silk factory, they recognized us, and a lady took us to another building, showing us the entrance. Another lady greeted us and said, "Tour," and we nodded. It cost three yuan (sixty cents each). We were handed a brochure in Chinese and English and started our tour. First was a display of silk worms, larvae, and cocoons. We learned it took seven cocoons to make one thread. Next was the design room, where artists were drawing and putting their drawings on graph paper. We saw men punching control cards for the looms, and it took one card for every thread line on the drawing. Manufacturing was next, where they were making the thread, and then on to watch the looms, where they were weaving the cloth that turned out silk pictures on the fabric. The last stop on the tour was the outlet store, where we bought some of the beautiful silk pictures and silk scarves. The clerks were holding hot water bottles to keep warm. The factory tour was so interesting especially to David, an old Georgia Tech industrial engineer. After we left the factory, we started walking back toward town and came upon a larger Friendship Store.

The second floor had the best silk prices we had seen in China. As I was looking at the silk, bright lights went on. I thought it was nice of them to turn on the light so I could see the fabric better. I looked around and saw cameras and lights shooting in my direction. I turned back and a girl came up and said they were taking pictures for TV tonight and needed my help. I went along with them and even started hamming it up a bit. The salesclerk pulled some bolts of silk off the shelf and put them on the counter. I unrolled some and held it up to my face to let David see if the color was good on me. We became TV stars overnight, or maybe we were being used for propaganda. It took me a little while to calm down from all this excitement and get serious about looking at the fabric. I bought four yards for a dress for me and four yards for my daughter-in-law. I noticed the hands of the clerk helping with the silk purchase and they were discolored, almost like they had been damaged from the cold.

We walked back to the hotel and ended a six-hour walking day. On the way back, we stopped in a little shop along the lake and got some ink stones at a very good price. Ink stone is Chinese in origin and used in calligraphy. It is a stone mortar for the grinding and containment of ink. The earliest excavated ink stone is dated from the third century BC and was discovered in a tomb located in Hubei province.

Back at the hotel, David went to pick up the airline tickets that he had left to be confirmed. He gave the girl a tract. I sat in the lobby waiting for David, and a baby ran toward me and stopped in front of me and started crying. I think the family was European and soon corralled the baby. A few minutes later a strange-looking person came in the hotel with something in front of him. I thought a street person had wandered in and was trying to sell something. Then more strange-looking people came in and I realized it was a tour group. I watched them with interest trying to figure out what this was all about. David returned, and he was taken back by the scene. As we left the lobby, we asked a bellboy who spoke English who these people were. He said that they were a group from Taiwan. The thing that shocked us was many of the people wore yellow aprons with a big pocket in front. Sitting in the pocket was a Buddha about one foot tall. The bellboy said that they carry their Buddha with them for good luck, just like Christians have Jesus. I told him that Christians do not have to carry around a stone god, because Jesus is alive and lives in our hearts.

We went to the Western restaurant for dinner. The entrance had a new look with a display of bunnies, chickens, little ducks and a sign saying Happy Easter. David asked the waitress if she knew what Easter was all about. She replied it was something to do with eggs and rabbits. David delighted to tell her about the real meaning of Easter. He gave her a tract when we finished eating. We enjoyed the Western food at the hotel. It is the best we had had in the six months we had been out of the United States. When we were leaving the restaurant, we saw some of the ladies from Taiwan coming down from the Chinese restaurant, and they were without their Buddha. They must have put him to bed.

The next day we were up at 6:00 a.m., and awoke to diarrhea and stomach pains again. I had a light breakfast and tried another one of those large white pills. We checked out and took a taxi to the airport. A crowd was already there, including another tour of Taiwanese, but they weren't carrying a Buddha. The area was so smoky that I almost choked. David got through the long ticket line and got seat assignments. We would learn after we got on the plane that we were in first class, a first for me. We went upstairs and through security and passport check required, even when you fly within China. We now made it to the next waiting room. I found a good buy on a large book about China and some postcards. We boarded the plane, and I wrote twenty postcards on the way to Guangzhou. I decided not to eat and to give my stomach a break for the day, hoping the pill would work. I drank a soda and had some more stomach cramps.

We flew over some small mountains and then into the clouds. We saw the ground again as we were approaching Guangzhou. We landed, disembarked out on the runway, and took a look at the crowded bus. There were so many people on it that the doors would barely close. We decided to wait for the next bus. We have noticed throughout China that the Chinese people all rush to be first in line or first on everywhere. They push and shove and walk over you to be first. I wonder if it is a fear that they are going to miss out on something and have fears that they will run out before they get there. Even waiting for the next bus, we ended up getting on last. That is probably good, because when the bus arrived at the terminal we just kind of got pushed off the bus by the people shoving behind us.

We had to exit the terminal and then walk around front to enter the Domestic Air Terminal again. We found a place to put our luggage, and I stayed with it while David went to inquire where we should go for our next flight. The place was crowded, noisy, smoky, and had no seats. We had about three hours to wait and really did not relish the idea of sitting on the floor. Later, we noticed just across the terminal was a window wall, and that area was the international air terminal. We thought maybe we could find someplace to sit there. We saw a man in uniform opening the sliding door in the wall. We grabbed our luggage and headed his way. We thought we looked like people who might be flying international, so maybe he would let us in. He was just closing the door as we approached, but reopened it for us to pass through. We saw an escalator going up to the shopping area, but it was not running. Then we spotted some seats behind the escalator; we sat there most of our waiting time. David went to check on the flight and discovered that there was an earlier one to Guilin. He spoke with a lady at the Supervisor's desk, and she said to come to that desk at 2:00 p.m. and wait. He thought she meant that if there were any extra seats on the flight that we could get them. My nose was clogged. I either had a cold or a sinus infection, or it was from the smoke all over China.

A little before 2:00 p.m., we gathered our luggage and went to the desk. David parked me and the luggage by a side wall and went to jostle the crowd in front of the desk. Soon, a very nice-looking, neatly dressed Chinese lady came and stood next to me. Before long she spit on the floor. It grossed me out, but I guess this is part of the culture. I had noticed all over China people blew their nose aiming for the floor and not using a handkerchief. A Chinese man once said, "Why would I want to put it in my pocket?" David returned to say that the plane was full and it was a small plane, so it was probably a good thing not to get on it.

We had been truly blessed throughout this trip. Our delay gave us more time to observe people. I told David that I was even beginning to like Chinese toilets. He said, "It's time for you to go home." I explained that I would rather have a dirty Chinese toilet in the floor than a dirty American toilet you sit on.

It was time for our flight and we noticed a line forming in front of the sign, so again David parked me with the luggage on the other side of the terminal and got in line. Even when you are next in line, people will push in front of you to get to the desk. It really appears to be a "push and shove" society. Space is not respected like it is among most Americans.

The desk finally opened, and David checked us in and got our seat assignments. We passed through security, through the passport check, and into the next waiting room. This one had seats, and David bought me a soda and a cookie. My stomach was beginning to feel better. We waited until almost departure time and then saw the plane with our number pulling in. David looked out the window and figured it would be boarding further down the terminal. They do not tell you what gate your plane will be boarding ahead of time, but announce it when it's time in Chinese. Then there is a great wave of people pushing and shoving to be first in line. We were trying to figure out ahead of time and not be left in the dust. We moved further down the terminal and then David noticed that it looked like the plane would be loading upstairs. We picked up our luggage and moved upstairs. We were carrying our luggage to avoid checking and claiming it at airports so not to lose it. We did not hear the plane announcement because it was in Chinese, but saw a great rush of people coming up the stairs. Even though we were up there first, we ended up boarding last for the hour flight to Guilin.

The taxis were more organized than in Hangzhou. They were all in a line, with a dispatcher who told us the flat rate to our hotel. Again, no meters were used. He made out a slip, and when we arrived at the hotel, the driver came in to the desk and had our name written on the paper. We wondered if the hotel got a cut. After checking in and getting settled in our room, we went to see about reservations for the boat trip on the Lijiang River, the main reason for our visit to Guilin.

The next morning, after a Western buffet breakfast, we went downstairs to wait for the bus that would take us to the boat. While we were waiting, we met Bob and Betty, a couple in their 70s from North Carolina. He was a dentist who had been selected by the American Dental Association to go to Hong Kong to work on the teeth of refugees for a month. We took a liking to them and invited them to visit us in Macau before they left Asia the end of the month. We also met an English lady named Olive who was in her mid-sixties and travelling all over Asia alone.

The bus came very late, but we were happy to see it had an English-speaking guide. It took about an hour to get to the Bamboo Harbor, where there were rows of large riverboats waiting. It was raining, and many of the vendors were selling plastic raincoats. We boarded one of the boats, and the lower level had rows of tables on each side, seating six people each. Each table had a white tablecloth and dishes of peanuts, candy, and snacks on it. There were two vendors selling souvenirs. We were not allowed to go to the top deck until the boat turned around and was underway. The boats took off in a line like a convoy. We went to the top and stood in the drizzle, and the scenery was spectacular.

We went back to our table for lunch and were asked if we wanted to buy extra dishes at US$10 to US$14 per dish. We just wanted whatever the tour included. When lunch was served, they placed a one-burner portable propane burner on each table and brought a pot of water or soup base with mushrooms, chicken, and some vegetables already in it. We were instructed that when it came to a boil to add the other items they had set on the table. There was fish with vegetables, beef, or maybe it was pork, and chunks of liver. They brought a pot of white rice, bottles of beer, and small boxes of chrysanthemum tea to each table. Oranges were served for dessert. Upon boarding, I had noticed the outdoor kitchen at the aft of the boat, and I took one look at the food and decided to stay on the top deck and look at the magnificent scenery. I had dreamed of this river trip for years. David opted to have lunch first and later told me how good it was. David always made the Chinese feel good by eating everything they served.

I stood on the top deck, amazed at the Lord's workmanship. There was a rainy drizzle through the five-hour trip, but it was worth it to see the beauty of the Lijiang River. There were sharp peaks, limestone that had worn away into a multitude of forms. Some were rugged, some rounded, some grown over with vegetation. Karst mountain ranges made of limestone and dolomite rocks rose over the river.

We went down the river past tiny villages, where I saw women washing clothes in the river. One was washing her chicken and vegetables for dinner. There were rafts on the shore made of bamboo with straw baskets in the middle. Young men, barefoot in the chilly water, would paddle out to our boat on a raft, rowing with timed strokes to intercept the boat, and tie alongside to sell their wares. They sold grapefruit, fish, and some had large fans, which they displayed through the boat windows to the people seated inside. We passed by water buffalo and other cattle along the shore. Ducks were swimming along the edge of the river. Cormorant birds were lined up in a row on bamboo rafts, waiting to be taken fishing. Chinese have been fishing with cormorant birds without the aid of a fishing rod since 960 AD. To control the birds, the fishermen tie a ring near the base of the bird's throat, which prevents them from swallowing any large fish but allows them to eat smaller fish with no discomfort. They release a cormorant that is very hungry, and it dives into the water, retrieves a carp, and returns to the raft with it.

Junks and sampans passed by. I saw farmers on terraced hillsides tending their plots, all manually cultivating. There were people walking on hillside paths with their baskets supported by bamboo poles from their shoulders. There were orange groves and peach trees in bloom. Camellias and forsythia were in bloom, too. Each turn around a bend of the river was a new experience; an adventure back in time. Small waterfalls flowed from the mountains.

We docked at Yangzhou and took the bus back to Guilin through a delightful valley surrounded by mountain crags. We made stops at an embroidery factory and an arts and crafts shop. Although they were interesting, we were barraged by the town's professional beggars. Olive told me she had seen the same group on the other side of Guilin when she took another tour. There was a man with no legs who sat on a tiny platform dressed in a suit coat, a one-legged man, and a blind man carrying a baby on his back. The baby never woke up and appeared to be drugged. I had learned seeing similar sights in other countries that this is one of the tactics beggars use. There was a young man with no shoes leading an old blind man around and practically dragging him from bus to bus. Our Chinese friends tell us that these are con games to play on one's sympathy, and begging is not necessary in China.

The next day we left the hotel, and the shuttle bus took us to the airport. There weren't too many people there when we arrived. The airport looked like it was out of an old movie, with a large scale to weigh luggage, a wooden shutter covered the check in window, a blaring TV, smoke everywhere. Smoking seems to be a main preoccupation of the Chinese. People smoked everywhere. It was hard to breathe with all the smoke. I surveyed the snack counter, and amidst the unknowns I saw a package of nuts and raisins and something that looked like a candy bar. I bought them just in case we would need dinner that evening.

We sat waiting for our plane, and as time moved on, David decided to position himself closer to the check-in window, especially when we saw a couple of people holding a fistful of passports and airline tickets. After a little while, he motioned to me, and I moved the luggage cart toward him. We continued to wait until the window opened. A very nice man reported that the incoming flight was delayed. If it could not land or take off again it would be cancelled. A little while later, a lady emerged with a piece of chalk and wrote cancellation on all the China Air flights. Ours was the only one listed under Dragon Air and was still on the board. The window opened again and David lined up. David struck up a conversation with a young man named Kevin from Singapore. He and his brother travel frequently in China for their commodity business. He spoke Chinese and English and was most helpful.

Our flight was cancelled because of fog, and Kevin told David to get in line to get his boarding pass for tomorrow. He also told David that Dragon Air was going to put us up in the Sheraton overnight at no charge. A woman with a fistful of tickets tried to get in front of David, and Kevin told her in Chinese to get to the back of the line. The Lord provided for us once again. David got the boarding pass and we climbed on the Sheraton bus for a return to Guilin. It was a five-star, the best hotel in town, and overlooked the Lijiang River.

The next morning, the shuttle bus took us back to the airport. It was still foggy, and we were doubtful that there would be a flight. All China Air flights were cancelled again. About 1:00 p.m., we heard the sound of a plane arriving, and it was ours. We eventually boarded and had a good flight back to Hong Kong. Arriving in Hong Kong, we claimed our luggage and were waved through customs. We caught a bus to the Macau Ferry Terminal. There were still tickets available for the 4:30 p.m. Jetfoil, which was leaving in a half hour. I went to call our missionary friends in Macau about our delay. By the time I figured out the phone, David was saying we needed to hurry. He had just remembered we needed to go through immigration before boarding the boat. We made a mad dash, praying all the way as minutes ticked away. They stamped our passports and our Olympic dash continued. We ran down the escalator through the waiting room, down the corridor and we finally made it: praise the Lord! There was an old man with a cane who was being helped across the ramp into the boat and that is what slowed the boat's departure. I could just imagine the Lord placing him there to buy us some extra time. We caught our breath as we looked out the window as the boat took off for Macau.

We learned when Bob and Betty came to visit us in Macau that they had been flying China Air and had a terrible story about their delay. They were put up in an awful Chinese hotel and the next day their flight was cancelled again. They spent another night in a worse hotel. They said they had a couple on their tour named Lord and Lady, who had tried to pull strings by making phone calls to the director of Dragon Air and everyone else they could think of. They could not get anyone to help them get out of Guilin and those bad hotels. Praise the Lord, we again saw His provision. Yes, Lord and Lady, it does make a difference whom you know.

I will lift up my eyes to the hills;
From where does my help come?
My help comes from the Lord,
Who made heaven and earth.
He will not let your foot be moved;
He who keeps you will not slumber.
Behold, He who keeps Israel
Will neither slumber nor sleep.

The Lord is your keeper,
The Lord is your shade on your right hand.
The sun shall not strike you by day,
Nor the moon by night.

The Lord will keep you from all evil;
He will keep your life.
The Lord will keep your going out
and your coming in
From this time forth and forevermore.
(Ps. 121)

Home sweet home—Back in Macau

Spring weather was damp and humid, and everything felt wet. The towels we used to shower were still damp the next morning, even if we hung them outside. I found mold growing on my leather shoes. Mildew formed on the ceiling and walls, especially in the bathroom. We had laundry to do from our trip to China. David had been helping with the laundry since we had been in Macau. We took the underwear, towels, and sheets to the "tattletale grey laundry" we found in the back of the photo shop. He did the rest in the bathtub, with lots of elbow grease, and hung them on our small balcony to dry. With the rainy season upon us, my black skirt was not dry a week later.

Our six-month short-term mission was drawing to a close, and we started making preparations to leave Macau. I needed a couple of dental crowns, and our missionary friends told us about a Chinese dentist who was trained in Canada. Dr. Pei put them both in for $450. I watched the Gulf War on TV while I waited in his office. We heard that Eastern Airlines had gone bankrupt and we were to fly with them from Dallas to Atlanta. We planned to stop and visit Craig and family in Dallas on our way back to Atlanta.

It seemed like a huge job to pack up and get back to the States. David borrowed some bathroom scales to check our luggage weight. We do not want to be overweight when we check in at Singapore

Airlines in Hong Kong. One of our Macanese friends helped us arrange with International Tourism for our luggage transport. We had five jumbo bags weighing sixty pounds plus carry-on luggage and other items. International Tourism would come to our apartment, take the bags to the Jetfoil, and put them on the boat. In Hong Kong, they would meet us at the boat and take the luggage downstairs to a van. We would be driven to the airport and dropped off in front with our luggage. Traveling overseas to live six months with a lot of luggage is a backbreaking job.

Good-byes have always been difficult for me. Vicky, our Chinese doctor friend, wanted to take us out to dinner with her husband and daughter. We went to a very old restaurant on the Square near the post office. We had chicken and shark fin soup, a cold dish of shrimp, vegetables and nuts, and a beef-and-onion dish. Then they served the specialty of the house, minced pigeon that you put in a leaf of lettuce, spread with plum sauce, roll, and eat. Vicky shared about difficult days during the Cultural Revolution in China. Being a doctor she was sent to the countryside to build a stone wall for re-education. She said, "Communism is hanging sheep head to buy the meat of dog. Capitalism is hanging dog head to buy the meat of dog." We talked about the meaning, and best I could understand was that Communist are liars. They talk a good story and use big dreams and big promises, but end up not coming through. Or, in the case of Vicky's metaphor, they promise the most expensive cut, but deliver bad meat. She felt in capitalism, what you speak about, you will get.

We talked about our trip to China and how everything looked like it was under construction or under repair. Even buildings that are completed have an unfinished look surrounded by leftover construction supplies and dirt instead of grass. Then we got talking about Jesus. She got all flustered when we talked about God. She said she believed everyone was the same when they died. She told about reading somewhere that Jesus was real in history and He was supposed to come down from the cross, but someone went and stabbed Him and this changed the history. I pray that the Lord will reveal His truth, and she will come to know the love of Jesus as Savior. "For God so loved the world, that He gave His only Son, that whoever believes in Him should not perish but have eternal life" (John 3:16).

Farewell dinners and more good-byes. We walked around the open-air market one more time. The market had always been a fun adventure. David was larger than the average Chinese, so when one vendor saw him coming, he would hold up clothing in David's size. One of his prize purchases was a pair of cotton pants with zippers on each leg to make them shorts. Another time in the market, David spotted a windbreaker hanging from the ceiling with a Master's emblem, and the label read Augusta National Golf Club. He wore that green jacket proudly for years. Macau was a manufacturing hub for many American and British companies. I noticed when I was in Beijing that Wen's gloves were very shabby, so I bought her a pair and went by the post office to mail them to her.

I had had a wonderful six months, but I was ready to go home. I was anxious to see friends, family, and be back at our church, First Baptist Church Atlanta. We had brought lots of Dr. Charles Stanley's tapes and given them away throughout this mission trip. I was looking forward to seeing what the Lord has planned for us as we return to Atlanta.

WHAT HAPPENS WHEN YOU PRAY BIG PRAYERS?

12

B ack at First Baptist Church Atlanta one Sunday morning, Dr. Stanley said, "We don't pray big enough." He challenged the congregation to ask God for something big, and then we paused to pray. Later, David and I compared our prayers, and we had both prayed for China to become a Christian nation. Just a short time after that, we received a call from Ming, who we knew from Friends from Abroad. She worked for an import/export company in Atlanta and asked for our help in organizing activities for a delegation that was coming to Atlanta from Mainland China.

We met with her and her employer, and they told us that forty mayors and deputy mayors from major Chinese cities were coming for a five-day visit. The delegation would also include top officials of the Communist Party and business people ranging from vice presidents to general managers of various industries, trading companies, banks, and high-tech companies. Imagine! We had just prayed big, and now we had an opportunity to perhaps change the opinion of Communist Chinese leaders about Christianity.

I asked the leadership of FBCA if they would partner in this endeavor. It took three months of planning to put together the five-day program. I learned that the delegates had a great interest in Atlanta's future hosting of the Olympics. China wanted to host the Olympics someday.

The visit began when we picked the delegates up in church buses at the airport. What a scene! Communist Chinese getting on buses marked FBCA. We posted signs in the front of the bus in Chinese: "No Smoking." During the three months of preparation, we formed a team comprised of several young couples with a heart for China who hoped to go there and live among the people. Some of them already had been to China and learned the language. They impressed the delegation by speaking Mandarin. Speaking a few words in someone's language says you care, and is an instant friendship builder.

The first event took place at Stone Mountain Park, where some of the 1996 Olympics would take place. Typical American picnic food was served at one of the park's pavilions. The Messenger Quartet, made up of four guys from FBCA, provided the entertainment. One of the delegates was so excited about the singing that he stood up and sang a song from his minority group. He was a Muslim from an unreached people group with no known church existing among them.

Many men and women from FBCA opened their businesses for the Chinese to tour. They shared how to operate a business incorporating business principles from the Bible. The Chinese were eager to learn and take back new ideas to their country. Some of the American business owners developed good contacts, which hopefully led to future trade with China. We arranged for someone from the Atlanta Olympic Committee to come to FBCA to speak to the Chinese. Remember, these were Communists who had never been in a church before.

Truett Cathy, founder of Chik-fil-A, hosted the delegation for lunch at his headquarters. He personally told them about being an American entrepreneur and how he started the fast food restaurants.

He gave each of them a copy of his book, which included his Christian testimony.

We put together a dinner with entertainment for the Mainland Chinese and charged Christian businessmen and women twenty-five dollars a plate to attend. This helped us fund the event. It was held in Fellowship Hall, where guests were seated at round tables. Each table consisted of a couple of delegates, four Christian business people, and interpreters from one of Atlanta's Chinese churches.

The master of ceremonies for the evening was Stan Cottrell, a church member and a long-distance runner. Shortly after China had opened up, Stan had done his "Great Friendship Run" across China. He started at the Great Wall north of Beijing and finished fifty-three days later 2,125 miles to the south in Guangzhou. Stan gave each of the delegates a copy of the book he wrote about his adventure. The Young Musicians on Mission sang. A touching moment was when the forty mayors sang China's national anthem.

I believe that these five days made an impact. The main Communist leader hugged me at the airport when he was leaving and said, "You good!" One of the delegates whose father was a vice premier of China before the Cultural Revolution, said during the visit, "Christians are love." My prayer was that all our new Chinese friends went home thinking a little more favorably toward the Church and Christians. This time could have a great impact on China!

We may not know results until we get to heaven. Invitations were issued to us by several Chinese mayors to visit them in their cities. Little did we know, we would soon have the chance to accept some of their invitations.

DELAYS AND DIFFICULTIES

13

D avid and I never planned to do so many mission trips. In fact, if the Lord had told us what was ahead of us back in 1987 when we said "yes, we'll go to Toronto," we might have run the opposite direction. We had completed three mission assignments, been blessed with the visit of forty Chinese mayors, and now we had settled back to our jobs at FBCA as administrative assistant and electrician. Actually, after all the exciting months of planning the mayors' visit, I was feeling a little bored and a thought ran through my mind: "Is it time to move on?"

One day, I got a call from the church receptionist that my boss had a visitor at her desk. I went up front to greet the person, and he was from Mainland China. He explained that he went to seminary in the United States and had founded a mission agency. He had a vision of taking used medical equipment into China and helping Christian doctors and nurses start clinics. We talked while waiting for my boss to come back from lunch. I told him about the mayors and our trips to China, Hong Kong, and Macau. After his meeting he came by my office and we talked some more.

It was only a few weeks later that I got a call from Tung, saying he would be in Atlanta for the weekend and wanted to meet with David and me. We had dinner with Tung and some of his friends, and he told us the medical equipment project was ready to begin. Would we pray about this vision and joining his mission agency?

During the next weeks, we enlisted some prayer partners to join with us as we sought the Lord's will. Tung had told us that we would be located in Hong Kong and make trips into China as needed. He said he had a Christian friend, Shen, who lived in Hong Kong and would be assisting us. Tung continued to give us more and more details about what we could expect working together on this project. We believed the Lord would have us go, and we were able to meet with Shen, who came over on a visitor's visa. Shen did not speak English, and we did not speak Chinese, which might be a problem.

By the end of 1992, we were on our way. Shen met us at the airport and helped haul our large bags to a taxi. Looking back, the series of trials ahead began when my feet hit the tarmac at the Hong Kong Airport. One of the first challenges that confronted us: where would we live? I couldn't know that the next three months would mean four moves and then an even greater trial.

We spent the first five nights in an eight-by-eight room in a guesthouse operated by Chinese Christians ministering in Mainland China. The walls were dirty and full of holes. A private bath was included, but I had to walk through the shower area to get to the toilet, a new concept for me. Jet lag numbed us from the initial culture shock. Our main goal was to get our sleeping schedule realigned to the thirteen-hour time zone difference. We were visited by two Chinese pastors who considered our welfare their responsibility. Rev. Yang took us to his home one afternoon and prepared dinner for us. He had a sweet, humble spirit, and it touched our hearts. He travels into China to preach, as well as to other areas of the world.

The other pastor told us that he was won to the Lord by Tung's witness seventeen years ago in China. He told us he had located a more suitable place for us to live. He put us in touch with another missionary, Joyce. We arranged to meet her the next day. We got off the train in the New Territories and found the spot where we would meet Joyce. She took us to a newly established guesthouse located only eight minutes from the China border. We could see small mountains with the border fence running along the top. This was indeed the countryside, but only an hour from the tall skyscrapers of Hong Kong Island. To get to our new residence, we had to take the subway, a train, and minibus. Once you got off the bus, you needed to be prepared for an adventure. We walked down a rocky path until we came to a chicken farmer's house, turned right, and continued on a path that was just six feet in front of hundreds of chickens. At the end was a wall made from corrugated steel roofing and a rusty door. As I walked down this path, I began to think, "Lord, I don't think I am hearing your leading right today." Reality quickly snapped my mind back, and wishing to persevere, I gave myself a quick rebuttal: "Be brave!" We walked through the door and into a sunny patio.

I noticed the washing machine was outside on the patio. It didn't look too bad now, and the view was great as I gazed up to the top of the mountain and one of the border guard stations. We were told that many try to escape from China each day over these mountains, and we could believe that was true, since our minibus to the farm had been stopped and searched by guards.

Inside the house were four bedrooms, a living room, a bath, and a kitchen. The bedroom furthest away from the chickens was ours. Our housemates were two young men who ran Bibles into China, and later we discovered they had some strange habits. At least, they seemed strange to me. One ate at least six cloves of garlic before he started his day and filled the whole house with a smell that nauseated me. I could live with that as long as I followed his path through the house with my can of Lysol. Lysol came in handy for the room of the other fellow, since he never cleaned it and left his clothing and all kinds of things on the floor. We were soon to learn who was providing snacks for the rats that lived in the house.

Unpacking and hanging posters, displaying some family pictures, and putting on a nice bedspread made it look a little more comfortable. Just simple touches, but I needed some reminders of home. Then came some of the hard adjustments: flies, which just came in and dropped dead, smoke from fires in the hills because of the lack of rain in the area, and the farmer who decided to burn off his field every night for a week. One evening I saw a flash; a mouse, a rat, I wasn't sure. No one else saw what I did. David assured me after a thorough search that it was not in our bedroom and I would be safe that night. I was so nervous to go to the bathroom that night. Well, I must trust God in all things, and that must include rats, too. Perhaps my scream had run him off and he wouldn't come back.

We planned to spend Thanksgiving with our friends in Macau and had our boat tickets. The night before we were to leave, I ran a high fever. David sent a fax to our prayer chain, who all must have prayed on the other side of the world while I slept. The next morning, I awoke with no fever. In fact, I slept all night, and I never felt the fever break. We were able to have a refreshing time visiting our friends.

We had sent a fax to one of the mayors who invited us to visit him in China. He sent back a warm welcome and said he would pick us up at the airport and make all arrangements for our visit. We would be able to combine this visit with the medical equipment project. The mayor arranged for us to meet with the administration at one of the best hospitals in the city. I will not mention the city we visited in order to protect our Chinese friends. I will just refer to it as "the city."

We flew into the city and were met at the airport by the mayor's secretary (male) and his driver. He arranged for our hotel for three nights as his guest. The next morning, we were picked up at the hotel and taken to the hospital and greeted by the hospital director, his assistant, and a representative from the health department. We climbed some metal stairs on the outside of the building and were escorted into a large conference room. We were served tea, the kind where the tea leaves get stuck in your teeth. They had plates of bananas, oranges, and apples on the table. They were most anxious to hear about the medical equipment proposal. There was no heat in the conference room and we soon learned there was no heat in the hospital.

We were given a tour of the hospital, and it was in sad condition. I told David if I got sick in China, he should fly me out or let me die, because I was not going to go to one of their hospitals. They told us the only heat in the hospital was in the intensive care area. When they took us into that area, a patient was just climbing back into bed with his winter jacket on. There were only two pieces of equipment in that unit, and they were both on a shelf. One was a monitor and the other a defibrillator. We were given hospital coats, masks, and a hat and taken into three operating rooms where surgery was being performed. We saw patients on cots in hallways, and lack of sterilization and basic equipment. The dental unit had three pots of water on a hot plate boiling for sterilization. They wanted us to install modern dental equipment and bring American dentists over to teach the latest technology.

Unfortunately, because of the tea, I needed to go to the restroom. One of the director's secretaries escorted me. The small room had two half doors. You stepped up, and there was a trough of running water going through the two cubicles. You guessed it; that was it. The weather was cool, so there was no smell, and I had learned to carry my own tissue. As I returned to the meeting, I passed by the accounting department and noticed they were using abacuses. I heard them invite us to stay for lunch, but after the tour and going into the operating rooms, I was not in the mood for lunch.

I saw the secretary looking at the metal bowls everyone eats out of and my imagination said, "She's getting us one of those unsterile metal bowls." We walked into the food service area and it was full of small, round tables, some still occupied by hospital staff, each with their metal bowl, and all over the tables were piles of bones. It looked like a disaster area. Chinese custom is to spit bones directly onto the table. I asked the Lord, "Am I going to be ushered to one of those tables and given my metal bowl?" I was thankful when they kept walking and took us into a small dining room with dishes and white tablecloths. I chose to eat just rice and vegetables. David again made everyone feel good, as he ate everything they offered.

That night, the mayor threw a banquet in our honor. The mayor had spent several days with us in Atlanta and knew we were Christians. He had the guests in two different rooms. He put the rowdy drinking, smoking group in one room, and the room we ate in there was no smoking. This is a rare thing in China, because everyone smokes everywhere. At our table was the assistant director of the hospital we had just visited. During the evening, he told us we could continue discussing our proposal, and we set up a meeting for Shen to come from Hong Kong and be included in the negotiations.

The next couple of days the mayor arranged for his driver and assistant to take us sightseeing. This was a good time for us to rest and get a little refreshed. One morning, we got up at the hotel and found the elevator not working. We learned it was our area's day to go without electricity. Thankfully it was only on the third floor. After one of the tours, we were taken to a small restaurant with a private room that had a window looking out on the parking lot. After ordering fish, rice, and vegetables, I looked out the window, and a man was cleaning our fish. He had it down on the asphalt driveway and was de-scaling it. I suddenly lost my appetite.

Our visit with the mayor came to an end, and the next morning Jen, our translator, met us and took us to a small university. They had a guesthouse, and it was not far from where she lived. We would stay there awaiting Shen's arrival from Hong Kong in about a week. It was December, and the temperature outside was in the thirties, and I am not sure it was much warmer inside. There was no heat, and we had many layers of clothing, but we still felt cold. David found some heavy drapes in a drawer and hung them at the windows. We prayed, "Dear Father, please keep us warm."

The guesthouse had a dining room where we ate our meals. The menu was posted each day on a blackboard in Chinese. There was a young lady who spoke some English to translate for us. The first night, we were served steamed rice, fish (full of bones), and two green vegetables. We were warned before going to China not to eat raw vegetables nor eat fruit if it wasn't peeled. They use human waste on their fields for fertilizer. After dinner, as we were walking back to our room, we sensed someone walking behind us. We turned around, and it was an old woman carrying a space heater. She wanted us to take it for our room, and it was probably the only heater in the place. Believe it or not, when we flushed the toilet that first night, it had hot water in it, and it never happened again during our stay. We laughed we could sit on the toilet and keep flushing to keep warm.

The next morning when we woke up, David said he would go plug the heater in, and we could stay in bed until the bathroom was warm. About a half hour later, we got up and learned that it was our area's day to do without electricity; so much for the space heater. We decided we would be warmer if we got outside. We wandered around the area and past a market where vendors were selling mostly vegetables. But we saw some live things in cages similar to those we saw outside a restaurant in Guangzhou. That's why, when in China, I become a vegetarian. We ate lunch at the guesthouse, and it was the same menu. When we went back for dinner that night, it was again the same menu. There was a new green vegetable, and I am sure it was clover. The next day, we made a run for a five-star hotel that had a small store with familiar items, like peanut butter. David said it was worth nine dollars for a small jar because it was his survival kit.

One of the last nights we ate at the guesthouse, the young lady who had been translating the menu lingered until everyone had left. We were just finishing our last bite, and she came to our table to talk with us. She asked, "Would you tell me something about Christmas?" Our hearts were about to burst. We had been praying for an opening. David ran to our room and came back with a Chinese Bible and a Gospel tract explaining the plan of salvation. She was eager to learn about the Bible and told us she had been to church once; in fact, it was last Christmas. I pray that when I get to heaven, we will meet up again.

Shen arrived, and after a short meeting with him and Jen, we went back to the hospital to continue our negotiations. We had prayed and had our prayer partners praying that there would be a oneness between Shen, Jen, and us and that there would be no confusion. We were relying on their translations to know what was going on. We are not sure what transpired, but no one in the room looked very happy. The best we could tell is that the medical people's demands were beyond what we could provide.

We were finished in this city for the time being and now checked flights to Hong Kong. We learned that there were no seats available until after Christmas. Disappointed, we sent a fax to our prayer partners to pray we could get out of China sooner. The next day, we checked back with the airline and found there were two seats available on a direct flight to Hong Kong the following day. Praise the Lord! I was so thankful for our prayer team.

When we returned to the "chicken farm," we hoped for a time of rest and revival from the trauma of China. But all we encountered were adversities. We believe Satan launched an all-out attack on us, and the next days were awful. They began with my expectation of getting a post office box, so we could hear from friends and family at home. We did not have an address yet, and we longed to get some news and words of encouragement from our prayer partners. It had been four and half weeks since we applied for the box, which was to take three. When we got back from China, I called and thought the man at the post office said the box had been approved and I should call back in two days. When I called back, I talked with the postmaster, who said he couldn't find our application, so we would have to reapply. I started to cry, little knowing that things were going to get worse.

The rat was back. In fact, every time David ran him out, he returned to his home under the refrigerator. The flies now were joined by gnats; they were all over the place and were not dropping dead anymore. The dreaded walk past the chicken farm got worse when I spotted a large dead rat one day and then another the next day. Each day as we passed the chickens and came near the farmer's house, his three guard dogs gnawed at the fence, growling and barking at us. One night after dark, we came down the road and were almost to the fence when my flashlight hit the eyes of the most feared dog, the pit bull that looked like he had mange. In terror, we realized he was outside the fence and standing just a few feet from us. We started screaming, "Get your dog," and the owner, who only spoke Chinese, ran out of his house and got it back inside the fence. We were able to communicate our fear without speaking the language. When I recovered, I asked David, "Have we been here two years yet, and is it time to go home?"

That incident was so frightening that I did not want to leave the house, especially after dark. Satan was out to discourage us, and he was doing a good job of it. I was ready to go home. David called the prayer chain at our home church, and they went to work and did a number on the evil one. We told our prayer chain that we could not stay there without their prayer support. They pray and we'll stay. They prayed us out of that bad situation and into a bright, quiet, and peaceful apartment. Shortly after they started to pray, we heard a missionary had an apartment for rent for two months. Another temporary solution, but we believed the Lord was again leading us. We moved into a nice two-bedroom, furnished apartment on the third floor of a village house in another area of the New Territories. It had a roof area where there was a washing machine and a covered place to dry clothes. The apartment belonged to a bachelor who had met another missionary at one of the Vietnamese refugee camps nearby and had gone home to Ireland to get married. They rented it to us for $130 per month. This apartment was comfortable and quiet, and I was able to recover from the trauma of the past weeks at the chicken farm. My nerves were still edgy as I passed dogs in the village, and I would jump if one barked at me. The days were filled with tests of everyday survival as we learned where to shop and what bus to take.

One Sunday morning, we took a minibus to the station where we could catch a double-decker bus to the subway and to Kowloon Tong. We wanted to find an English-speaking church, and a computer salesman told us about one he attended. This particular Sunday, we were off on a two-hour trip to an English-speaking international congregation within a Chinese church. We had the address but miscalculated exactly where it was on this long street. We walked for what seemed miles, and by the time we got there, church was almost over. They had a social time following the service on the patio, and we met several Americans who were there on business assignments. We met Chinese and Filipinos and some Australians and Europeans. A young Chinese fellow who heard we were from Atlanta came up to say hello. He said, "I'm Samuel. So you are from Atlanta? Do you know Larry Ragan at First Baptist Church Atlanta?" Larry was assistant mission director at our church, and Samuel and Larry had been roommates at Dallas Theological Seminary. Samuel also knew an American missionary who was best friends with the missionary we had served with in Macau. It is a small world with a big God. We met Pastor Milford who invited us for dinner after the service the next Sunday.

The next Sunday, we got to the church on time and enjoyed having dinner and fellowship with Pastor Milford and his wife after the service. He told us that longtime church members there knew very little basic theology. Other believers were dabbling in things that are of the spirit world, such as meditation, Oriental breathing exercises, counseling with ungodly counselors, fortunetellers, New Age, and other forms of the occult. Add all those together with the uncertainty of the future Communist takeover of Hong Kong, and one can see lots of needs for a good Bible-teaching church.

We continued to attend that church throughout our stay in Hong Kong. Several weeks later, the pastor asked me to teach a ladies' Sunday school class. There were thirty-six ladies in the class who were predominately Chinese and Filipinos. I taught a favorite book of mine, *Classic Christianity* by Bob George. After class one day, a Chinese lady told me she was seeing a counselor and was so discouraged that she had been planning how to commit suicide. She said this book helped her to see her identity in Christ and have hope.

We were enjoying the quiet village, and recovering from culture shock. Walking around the village we began to inquire about apartments for rent. We looked at several empty places but still had several weeks to remain in our comfortable temporary home. One day, when we were out exploring, we found a new village house that consisted of three floors. Neighborhood children helped translate as we asked their mother about the availability of the house. Before we knew it, they had telephoned the owner, and he was on his way over. The house was wonderful, and we thought that this must be the place that the Lord had selected for us. The owner told us it would not have water until early February, which would be fine, since we could stay in our temporary home until then.

We continued to pray about the house until one day we heard the missionary would be returning earlier than expected. When we called the owner of the house we had looked at, he stated that he was going to rent it to relatives, instead. We were so disappointed and continued to question where the Lord wanted us to live. A missionary friend told us of a place across from him, and we went to look at it. It was a new house, but for some reason we did not feel comfortable there. We were getting accustomed to life in this little village and didn't really want to leave.

The next morning, we got up and walked around the village, asking the Lord where He wanted us. We looked at all the empty places and were about ready to head back home. I started walking toward the middle of the village, and David said he didn't think there was anything in that direction that he would be interested in renting, since most were very old buildings. "Let's go this way," he said, and we headed toward the left. There was a new house on that path that we had seen many times, but never saw anyone in it. Just as we passed by, an old man came out of the door. He did not speak any English and our Chinese only consisted of a few words, but we were able to communicate that we were looking for a place to live. He gave us a tour of the three floors; each floor had a three-bedroom apartment. We ended up renting one of the apartments.

Praise the Lord; we finally would have a permanent place to live. Our new apartment was toward the back of the village called Water Tail Village, while our temporary apartment was up front in Water Head Village. They say that this signifies the position of the river, but we had only seen a small, polluted stream, although it must turn into a river in the rainy season, because we heard there was flooding last spring. We were warned not to live on the first floor because waist-deep water had poured through the village. Homes in this village are owned by the Tang family, which goes back to the Tang dynasty. We were told that the government must give each male Tang a piece of property to build a house, and it creates extra homes being built for investment. I guess they wanted to get them built before the Communist China takeover.

Apartments in this part of the world come with four walls, and you are responsible for the purchase and installation of the water heater, air conditioners, stove, refrigerator, etc. The walls are concrete, so you must drill every hole in order to even hang curtain rods. David did enough honey-dos to last him for years.

Our apartment was located on the third floor and had a large balcony in front. A few weeks before, we had purchased some furniture from a missionary who lived in the village and was going to Mongolia. They kept it until we could move it to our new apartment. David and the missionary devised a pulley system so they could pull the items up to the third floor and then lift them over the balcony railing. The timing was good, because it was Chinese New Year and it was a tradition to thoroughly cleanse the house in order to sweep away any ill-fortune and to make way for good incoming luck. Some people even threw furniture in the dumpster. We went dumpster diving, and among the red Buddhist altars that were tossed out making room for their new altar with new gods, we found a wood framed sofa. Later, I was able to find wide sheeting material and filling and made a cushion that was semi-comfortable.

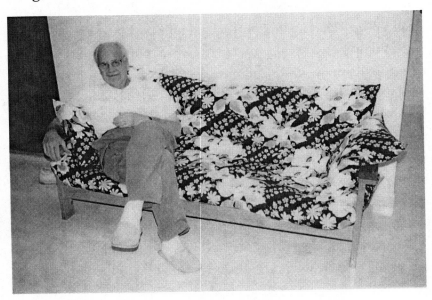

We were given twin beds by a Chinese doctor who was moving to California. We put them together and it made a king-size bed and filled the bedroom. I mean literally filled the bedroom that was nine and a half by seven and a half. We had to crawl in bed from the foot, but we would never fall out of bed, because we were surrounded by three walls. And this was the master bedroom; the other two bedrooms were seven and a half by seven and a half.

We have been trying to get used to village life and living in a cement building with no central heat. It was rainy and cold. We bought a small electric heater, and we wore lots of layers of clothing. We also bought a radiator-type heater filled with oil. Unfortunately, the bathroom window needed to stay cracked because of the propane hot water heater, so there was always some cold air coming in.

I was thrilled to have an apartment-size stove with an oven, but learning to shop and cook was a challenge for me. David had a large shoulder bag that he carried everywhere we went. We called it the trunk of our car even though our travel was on buses. When we passed a store, we would dash in to see if they happened to have something that looked familiar. In this part of the world, shipments would come in for a particular item, and then you might never see it again. On a recent trip to Hong Kong Island, we had purchased some ricotta and some lasagna noodles. I had visions of an Italian dinner. I opened the box of pasta and emptied it into the boiling water, and then I saw bugs swimming on top. It went into the garbage, and I revised the menu to mock-lasagna using some elbow macaroni I had on hand. I finished the casserole, and when it was time to put it in the oven, the oven wouldn't work. That was the way it went here. There was always one more problem and one more challenge to overcome. I felt depressed as I remembered the lovely little kitchen I had in Atlanta.

I finally was learning how to shop and cook so I could venture to entertain. We invited Rev. Yang to visit. He was the Chinese pastor who helped us when we first arrived. He was cold, so we placed him near a heater. It was the first heater he had been near all winter, and I felt so selfish about my American expectations. We served him dinner and put on some praise music and he fell asleep. I had a lot to learn about sacrifice.

I still had not cooked any meat yet. When I thought I wanted some meat, I went to the market and looked at it hanging out in the open, and then I remembered why I wanted to be a vegetarian in Asia. The best thing was bringing some spices with me so I could get the taste of home. I cook meatless chili, pasta, beans, and even black-eyed peas. David, a Southern boy, loves black-eyed peas and cornbread. I found some cornbread mix in one of the stores. I made a meatless stew once and used a can of Campbell's Ox Tail Soup for flavoring. It was good, and I made dumplings from a box of Bisquick.

The stove we bought from a missionary ran on propane gas. It had four burners and an oven that didn't work. David, an engineer, diagnosed the problem as a bad thermocouple. He removed it and carried it around in his pocket for a couple of weeks. Everywhere we went, he would pop into a shop, show it, and ask if they had one. Most only laughed and shook their heads. One Saturday, we were determined to find one and spent five hours with no results. When we got home, I said, "Why don't you put the old one back in and try it again? Maybe God healed it while you were carrying it around." He took my emery board and polished the end, and praise the Lord—a healed oven. I said, "We have to pray for everything here." I think that is what the Bible says. But in our less complicated life in the USA, it seems like there are things I could do without stopping to pray. I could jump in the car and go to the store and have a choice of twenty different versions of the item I wanted.

I thought I was getting over culture shock and beginning to settle in. I was thinking I didn't know how to do anything and wasn't even sure I liked the people we came to minister to. That really is culture shock. Even a simple thing like going to the restroom was a problem. I told David one day that I didn't know the restroom rules in this culture. I would go into a restroom and stand behind the last lady who was waiting, like I would do in the USA. Then some Chinese ladies would come in and walk right past me, and to be honest it would make me mad. I think I figured out the system. You go in and bet on a stall. You try to figure out which one will be empty first. You stand directly in front of that one and rush in as soon as the other lady opens the door. Oh, my dear lady friends, have I gone completely out of my mind? David and I joke about being "invisible" as people pushed past us in lines.

One night, we came back to our little village after dark, and as we were walking down the road, a minibus came by and we hailed it and got on. It ran periodically and was a way to get to the back of the village where we lived. I am *so* glad we were on it. Up the road, we came upon a herd of water buffalo, about twenty of them. They were in the road, on both sides, and in the tall grass next to the little stream. There were big ones, newborn, and all the sizes in between. They seemed confused by the bus lights. I would have absolutely lost it if I had been walking up the road and stumbled upon them. Just last week, we had walked up this road and turned a corner and looked right at two big water buffalos staring at us.

Sometimes I wondered, "Why we are here?" We spent each day just trying to survive and did not seem to be doing any real ministry. We spent our time waiting for doors to open. Our time in China was a trial, and I did not look forward to the next trip there. I'd been frightened by so many things here, including these water buffalos. Psalm 88:3 states, "For my soul is full of troubles..." It is only that God reaches down and pulls me out of the pit of despair and fills me with His peace that I continue on.

We had learned that Alistair Begg was coming to Hong Kong for the week of Keswick Convention. The timing was perfect because we needed a week of refreshment as we listened to him teach on Daniel. These spirit-filled weeks of Bible teaching started in Keswick, England, in the early 1800s. The founder of the China Inland

Mission, Hudson Taylor, spoke at one of them, and in response Amy Carmichael decided to dedicate her life to missions. She was a missionary to India among orphaned children. One of her quotes reads:

We say, then, to anyone who is under trial, give him time to steep the soul in His eternal truth. Go into the open air, look up into the depths of the sky, or out upon the wideness of the sea, or on the strength of the hills that is His also; or, if bound in the body, go forth in the spirit; spirit is not bound. Give him time and, as surely as dawn follows night, there will break upon the heart a sense of certainty that cannot be shaken.[4]

Settling in was a lot of work, but we rejoiced in having a permanent place of our own. The two-year lease had been signed and the last curtain made and hung. Then a blow we had not expected came. Some missionaries had told us Americans are always welcome and can come and go in Hong Kong. Since we would be spending a great deal of time in China, we understood that we could come to Hong Kong on a visitor's visa for thirty days with no problem. Each thirty days, we would need to leave the country and come back in. Our project in China had been delayed, and we had done several trips in and out of Hong Kong, and each time they stamped our passport. This particular month, we made one of our visa exit trips from Hong Kong to Macau. When we came back in, I went first and got thru immigration and was walking along, and I realized David was not behind me. I looked back, and he had been detained at the checkpoint. He was told that he could not continue doing that and would have to leave after the next thirty days.

We had been in Hong Kong just a few months, and it seemed like forever. We had lived in three different places and travelled in China. These have been the longest weeks of my life. The trials had been many, and I was worn down and ready to go home. I'd been ready so many times during these months. "Where do you want us, Lord? If you want us to go back to our comfortable home in the USA, we would be happy to do so." But then the thought crossed my mind that the Lord might want us live in China. Oh, how difficult that would be. But I know the only way to true happiness is trusting the Lord and surrendering, so I gave up my rights to where I should live and surrendered to living in China if that was what He wanted.

The next weeks were full of prayer and counseling with people who knew the immigration laws. After several phone calls we learned that we must go to a country where there was an American Embassy and a British Embassy. The closest place would be Manila, in the Philippines, about a two-hour flight from Hong Kong. We got our airline tickets and made reservations to stay in a missionary guesthouse. Our goal was to get a new American passport, because we had to get one that was free from all the Hong Kong entry stamps. Then, once we had a new passport, we had to get a three-month visa from the British Embassy in order to live in Hong Kong.

Once in Manila, we headed for the American Embassy. We made our request and told the truth about our entries into Hong Kong. The official looked at us and said, "Well, I don't think you are drug dealers, so I will grant you a new passport." Praise the Lord, one down and we then headed to the British Embassy. We asked for an application for a visa and took it back to the guesthouse to fill it out. Oh my, the questions were things like, "How many times have you been to Hong Kong? What are your most recent dates? Do you have a round-trip airline ticket for Hong Kong?" The more we read, the more we realized that if we told the truth we probably would not get a visa. We prayed and felt we had to tell the truth. We filled it out, went back, and turned it in. We were instructed to come back the next afternoon at three o'clock. Back to prayer and more prayer.

When we returned the next day, we were almost breathless as our name was called and we approached the counter. We were granted the visa. Whew! We were exhausted from the stress and called time-out and spent a week resting.

Our missionary friends in Macau had been to this area of the Philippines and told us about a local beach resort on the next island and how to get there. The next day, we checked out of the guesthouse and boarded a local bus for Bantangas City at the south end of Luzon, the same island Manila is on. At Bantangas City, we took a ferry across to Puerto Galera on the island of Mindoro. When the ferry docked, our friends told us to walk to the end of the pier and turn left. At the end of that street, we would find jeepneys and should ask which one went to Tamara Beach. Jeepneys are a popular means of transportation. They were originally made from US military jeeps left over from World War II. The name is a combination of *Jeep* and *knee* because the passengers sit very close to each other. They are colorfully decorated, and the back open air portion has a row of seats on each side.

We found the right one, and the driver tossed our luggage on top along with the chickens in cages and baskets of vegetables. We soon learned that we needed a towel to cover our faces as we went down the dirt road with the dust blowing inside the jeepney. We had asked the driver to tell us when we got to Tamara Beach. We made several stops, and then we heard our destination called. We were on a dirt road, and there was a little sign nailed to a tree with an arrow pointing toward Tamara Beach. The driver got our luggage off, and we headed down the path. We knew from our friends that this local resort did not have a telephone to make reservations. We had arrived on faith that they would have room for us, and praise the Lord there was one room left. Actually, it was a little bamboo hut with a small porch on the front. There was a wooden platform that was the bed. I guess you were supposed to bring your own bedroll. We stepped down to the bathroom. There was a pail to use to flush the toilet, and the shower water temperature depended on what time of day it was. The hut was right on a beautiful beach, and there was an open-air restaurant that served marvelous fish meals.

Our first task the next day was to look for something to make our bed feel more like a bed instead of a log. We walked through the little town and spied an air mattress displayed. We bought two, and that night we blew them up. Now for a good night's sleep. Well, about midnight, we woke up with both mattresses deflated, and we were back to sleeping like a log—no, on a log.

During the day, we swam in the wonderful blue water. Our beach was separated by a pile of large rocks from the next beach. Sometimes Filipino ladies would climb over the rocks and come on our beach selling mangoes. They were the best mangoes I have ever eaten. On Palm Sunday, we sat on those rocks, and some of the ladies came and joined us. David read from Luke 19:40, where Jesus said,

"I tell you if these [meaning his disciples] were silent, the very stones would cry out!" I'll never forget that visual message! We had Gospel tracts to give. We pray we will see these ladies again in heaven.

The week on Tamara Beach was a week of rest and refreshment, and the meals were great at the little restaurant. We had noticed outrigger canoes parked on the beach and asked the owner of the restaurant about getting a ride along the coast in one of them. He was able to arrange for a full-day tour for twenty dollars. An outrigger canoe is a type of canoe with a lateral support fastened on each side. This kind of prevents the canoe from tipping over, at least we hoped. Our guide took us along the beautiful beaches for miles, and we put into a little resort area for lunch. It was a boat trip of a lifetime. At the end of our week at Tamara Beach, we felt refreshed, and it had only cost around four hundred dollars for everything. We felt we could face going back to Hong Kong and even China.

Back to Hong Kong with a three-month visa, and we sailed through immigration with no problems. We got word from our mission leader that no agreement was reached at the Chinese hospital we had visited. They wanted more than we could deliver. However, there was a request from another hospital for ten dialysis machines. He thought this might lead to a joint venture for a dialysis center in China. David was to connect with a hospital in Hong Kong that had similar equipment and check on installation and operation manuals. We now had hope that finally the mission we had come for would begin.

We're learning more about trusting Him for everything. The visa trip to Manila had been a drain on our finances. Missionaries living overseas like us need a point person in the USA to send out prayer letters, and handle mail and banking. Our friend Judy had volunteered to be our point person. After months living in Hong Kong, we counted our money and we had very little left, with about two weeks to go before our monthly check arrived. We had expected a five-hundred-dollar refund from an insurance company after we left the USA, but that was several months ago. We called Judy, hoping that check had arrived and was now in our personal checking account. Judy recalled the check coming but thought it had been sent on to our mission account and it would be included in our regular monthly check. A few days passed, and we received a call from our coworker, Shen, saying he had some mail for us. We would meet him after church on Sunday at the Kowloon Tong train station. Our hopes went up again. We had enough money left to get to church, but not quite enough to get back home. God is Sovereign, and He knows what He is doing. We trusted Him to come here because we believed that was His will, and He had promised to take care of us. Could we trust Him now in this situation?

We went to church, and when the offering plate was passed, David dumped the last few coins in. Now our pockets were empty. David planned to borrow a little from Shen so we would have bus fare home. I had visions of someone at home enclosing a five-dollar bill in one of their letters. That would take some pressure off. We met Shen at the appointed time, and while David and Shen talked, I ripped open all the letters from home. No time to read the most welcome news and encouragement; the search was on for greenbacks. Well, you guessed it, sweet notes from friends and family, but no money. David borrowed HK$100 (about US$12) from Shen, and we headed back to the countryside where we lived. On the bus, I opened the large envelop from Judy with all kinds of business items enclosed. And then, there it was—a check stub from that insurance company with a note on it that over five hundred dollars had been deposited in our Atlanta checking account. We did have money; we just didn't know where it was. Praise the Lord for Judy. The Lord used her to keep me on the ragged edge. Learning to lean, yes, that is what it all about.

Monday morning, I looked out the balcony window and saw the strangest sight: a Buddhist funeral was taking place in the field across from us. There were people dressed in white robes with pointed hats, and they looked somewhat like the Ku Klux Klan. I saw a paper house being burned. I understand that joss paper and prayer money are burned to ensure that the spirit of the deceased has lots of good things in the afterlife. Praise the Lord that those who have trusted in Jesus as Savior have the assurance found in John 14:1–6: "'Let not your hearts be troubled. Believe in God; believe also in me. In my Father's house are many rooms. If it were not so, would I have told you that I go to prepare a place for you? And if I go and prepare a place for you, I will come again and will take you to myself, that where I am you may be also. And you know the way to where I am going.' Thomas said to Him, 'Lord, we do not know where you are going. How can we know the way?' Jesus said to Him, 'I am the way, and the truth, and the life. No one comes to the Father except through me.'"

As the weeks went by, we learned of one delay after another, and then we heard that the first container of used medical equipment was on its way and due to arrive at a Chinese port in a couple of months. But these delays in the project prevented us from going into China. We also learned that the dialysis center project was abandoned because those involved in China did not pursue the proper steps for approval. Our mission leader had found another group to enter into an agreement, but this means more delay before we could go into China. Although early approval had been promised, based on past history, we couldn't count on it happening soon. The first group heard about the new agreement, and they were now saying they wanted to be the first and showing renewed interest. Confusion! We were told that a group from western China flew to meet with our representatives and signed a preliminary agreement for equipment. They, too, promised approval soon, but until proper approval was obtained, we could not count on it. When negotiating with China, there was always a big question in one's mind, even when you have the proper approval. Remember, this was a pioneer mission project being done in a Communist country. This was a new mission agency and we were the first non-Chinese to join them.

What should we do? Stay here and wait it out? Our three-month visa time was ticking away, and when it was up, we would have to leave the country to obtain another one. That involves more expense. Should we return to the USA, where David could get additional medical equipment training, and I could assist in the organization of a multitude of future projects that are in the planning stage? Or is the

Lord closing this door? There are many potential projects that made the future work in China look very promising, but the immediate question was, "What should we do now?" Our prayer partners were enlisted to help us discern what the Lord was saying. An old Kenny Rogers song came to mind: "You got to know when to hold 'em, know when to fold 'em and know when to walk away." After much prayer and counsel, we decided it was time to walk away.

Before returning to Atlanta, one of our prayer partners, Joann, invited us to come and stay with her until we could get an apartment. We accepted her gracious offer. We began the process of getting rid of all our furniture and breaking our lease. It took so much energy to finally get settled. Several missionaries were blessed when we gave them our household furnishings. We flew back to Atlanta and climbed into bed at Joann's on Sunday, June 27. David was able to get his job back at First Baptist Church Atlanta and started work on July 1. By July 3, we had purchased a car and signed a lease for an apartment, but couldn't move in until August 6. Everything seemed to be falling in place.

Three days later, on July 6, I learned that Joann's brother was coming to visit on the ninth. Since the only place left for him to sleep would be on the small love seat, I realized we needed to find another place to stay. I prayed that morning and read in Proverbs 16:9: "The heart of man plans his way, but the Lord directs his steps." I cried to the Lord, "Where Lord, where can we live until August 6th?" Almost immediately I was reminded of Psalm 32:8 says, "I will instruct you and teach you in the way you should go; I will counsel you with my eye upon you." I thought, "Lord, I am so tired of moving and having constant change, but I accept this new development as coming from your loving hand. I count on your direction to be clear and, I hope, quick. I don't want to hang out on a ledge long, but I yield to your every direction." Psalm 31:7–8, "I will rejoice and be glad in your steadfast love, because you have seen my affliction; you have known the distress of my soul, and you have not delivered me into the hand of the enemy; you have set my feet in a broad place." I cried, "Where is the large, broad place, Lord?" That same day, I went into the First Baptist Missions Office, and they had just received a call from Michael and Michele offering for a missionary to come stay with them in their large house in Alpharetta. Amazing how fast the Lord answered. A day before Joann's brother arrived, we moved to Michael and Michele's lovely large home. Michael was an investment advisor and worked out of his home. Praise the Lord! How good He is to us! Not only did Michael and Michele provide us temporary housing, but they were spiritual encouragers and soon to give great investment counsel.

MORE SURPRISES COMING

14

My job hunting took a turn that I had not expected. Since the time we had returned from our first mission assignment, I had always gone to work at FBCA following a mission trip. This time, when I returned, there was a new personnel director. I interviewed with him, and he looked at my résumé and said he thought it looked like I was unstable, moving around so much. I told him that, before I started obeying God, my résumé looked very stable. He said he did not have any place for me at that time. Someone told me they saw an opening at Mission to the World, part of the Presbyterian Church of America (PCA). I checked it out, and it was for administrative assistant to the executive director, John Kyle. He was retiring and needed an interim assistant. I applied and went through a battery of tests, including a typing test. It was the first time in my life that I typed eighty words per minute. I got the job, and what a privilege it was to work for such a godly man as John Kyle. John had been with Intervarsity for years and with Wycliffe. During my time with him, I was asked to take minutes at the annual board meeting, and it was a special experience to meet other mission greats like Luis Bush. Luis was international director of the AD2000 & Beyond Movement which later became known as the Joshua Project. Luis coined the term "10/40 Window" that focused on the region of the world with the least exposure to Christianity. I gained so much insight into world missions through this temporary assignment. It was just the encouragement I needed after my time in Hong Kong and China. About the time this assignment was drawing to a close, there was an opening at FBCA.

It was great to be back among friends and family. We got involved in Friends from Abroad again and enjoyed entertaining in our apartment. It was so easy with a full kitchen. Chuck was home from teaching English in China and had married a Chinese girl. They came by and brought their baby. Soon they were off to teach in Saudi Arabia. During this time in Atlanta, David's mother died at age ninety-five and left a small inheritance to David. David sought investment counsel with Michael.

There was a point we went for some counseling with a man named Jeff, who was with Navigators. We had had our first experience with "sheep bite." You know, when you hang out in the sheep pen long enough, some well-meaning Christian might bite, and it hurts. During one of those counseling sessions, Jeff asked if I had come from an alcoholic family. I told him not that I knew of and I wanted to know why he asked that question. He said that so much of what I described in my childhood years sounds like experiences that a child of an alcoholic would have. After that session, I asked the Lord to show me if there was anything hidden in my past.

Well, maybe I should have begun my story with my early years. I was born a farm girl outside of Gainesville, New York. I don't have many memories of those early years, only what people have told me. I guess I grabbed those as memories.

My dad, Harold, and mother, Eleanor, lived on the farm in one part of a duplex, with my dad's parents living in the other half. My mother's parents lived across the road on another farm. My dad worked the farm and served the other farmers by picking up their milk cans and driving them to the dairy. Maybe you have seen some of the antique milk cans that people decorate and put on their front porch. The farmers would put their full milk cans out on the edge of the road and my dad would come along and pick them up. He would return their cans the next time he picked up another load.

One snowy day in January 1943, a couple of months before my fourth birthday, he had made his round picking up the cans and was headed for the dairy. I've always heard my dad was a kind, gentle man and always willing to help a person in need. This day was no different when he saw a truck off the road stuck in the middle of a snow blizzard. He parked in front of that truck and was putting on chains to pull it out of the ditch. Another truck blinded by the snowstorm hit the rear of the disabled truck and my dad was crushed and killed.

It had been only months before that my grandfather, my mother's father, had a stroke while sitting in his chair and died. Less than four years old, and I was now surrounded by a grieving mother and grandmother. Add two widowed aunts and you have my four playmates until I was the age of eight. I guess that is why I feel I was never a child, just a little one surrounded by grown-ups.

I lived with my grandmother in Warsaw, New York, and my mother went to work in Rochester. She would come home on weekends. One Saturday, she came home and found both me and my grandmother passed out on the floor. We had been overcome by gas from a hot water heater. That was back before they put a harmless chemical into it to give it an odor.

We survived, but the doctor recommended that we spend the winter in Florida to help get the gas out of our lungs. The first year my mother took us, and the second year she sent my grandmother, two aunts, and me down to the Tampa area. While we were there, my mother married a man who I had never met. So much in my life spelled rejection. For years, I felt there was a war going on between my mother and me. I could not figure out why an only child would feel so much rejection. I thought the only child was usually pampered and spoiled.

On the last day of August, I worked late at FBCA. David got home before me, and after dinner he told me he had received a call from a man who proceeded to tell him an incredible story. The man, Bill, lived in Connecticut and had been adopted at birth. He said while his adopted mother was living she would not tell him anything about the adoption, and he said he really didn't care because he had great parents. However, on her death he found an envelope that provided details about the adoption and the name given to him by his birth mother. After reading the details and sharing it with his children, the decision was made to see if they could learn any information about their blood relatives. He hired someone to search the trail and it led to me. His birth mother's name was the same as my mother's name. He was born when she was sixteen years old.

I spent the next twenty-four hours in shock. Then I called my aunt, who was in her eighties, and asked, "Can this be true?" She replied, "I'm afraid it is."

Bill and I talked several times and exchanged pictures. On September 20, he and his wife, Rita, came to Atlanta for our first meeting. It was a most unusual feeling to meet a person who had some of my same features, and as we got to know each other, we could see personality traits that were similar. He was born in Westchester, PA, in 1931. My aunt confirmed that my mother and grandmother had left home in late November or early December, 1930, under the pretense that my mother was going for treatment of Bright's disease. Incidentally, all my life I had put down Bright's disease on family medical history forms, when it was actually for the birth of my half-brother. My aunt moved her wedding date up and got married that December to my mother's brother in order to go over to the farm to keep house while my grandmother was away.

Bill was adopted by a New Jersey couple at a hospital in Westchester, near Philadelphia. His birth name was listed as David Lee, and that is the name my mother had told me for years I would have been named if I were a boy. Bill worked in New York City with a radio network and had three children and four grandchildren. He still ran marathons at the age of sixty-three. I told him I run for the bus when I'm forced to.

Our first meeting took place at First Baptist Church Atlanta, and it was videoed. It is difficult to express the feelings involved in meeting a brother who I never knew existed. David picked Bill and Rita up from a hotel and brought them to our meeting. I knew it was about time for them to arrive, and I heard voices coming toward the office door. I knew when I opened the door I would be looking at my brother for the first time. I opened it, and he greeted me with a big hug. I said, "I am glad you found me." I experienced God's grace and peace during our first meeting and throughout those extremely emotional weeks.

The second evening we were together, Bill led the conversation head on into spiritual things. He asked about the type of counseling I did, and I was able to share how Jesus saved me when I was thirty. He had many questions and would ask three more questions before I could finish answering one. At dinner, he shared that he had a void in his life and did not know what would fill it. His wife stated that she felt the same way. I knew nothing would fill the void except Jesus.

In the years to come, we visited Bill and Rita in their home and met their family. We keep in touch from time to time. This event of a half-brother coming out of nowhere explained a lot to me about my mother. I could understand her better: the buried guilt, the loss of her first husband, and how she blamed God. After I came to the Lord at the age of thirty, I shared the Gospel with her and she admitted to making a decision for Christ at the age of sixteen.

I think I was learning more about God and His provision whether I was in Hong Kong or Atlanta. Life is a training ground, and God's plan is first to bring us to Himself and then grow us up to be more like Jesus.

"For by grace you have been saved through faith. And this is not your own doing; it is the gift of God, not a result of works, so that no one may boast. For we are His workmanship, created in Christ Jesus for good works, which God prepared beforehand, that we should walk in them" (Eph. 2:8–10).

HONG KONG: SECOND TIME AROUND 15

O ur next trip to Hong Kong was to work at the church we had attended previously. I was to be the administrative assistant to the pastor of the International English Speaking Congregation and a missionary. David was to help develop a small group ministry plan.

The church arranged for an apartment nearby in Kowloon City. It was a third floor walk-up in the flight path of the airport. There were building height restrictions imposed in Kowloon City for air traffic approaching the old Kai Tak Airport. Our building was in that three-floor corridor, and on each side were high-rise buildings. We could stand on the roof and wave to incoming passengers on low flying planes. The pigeons on the roof were so used to the noise that they didn't even flinch.

Some of our greatest blessings while in Hong Kong were the guys from Nagaland who were at a drug rehab on Dawn Island in the South China Sea. This drug rehab was started by a Chinese pastor, Rev. John Paul Chan. He told us that years ago he would walk past Kowloon's Walled City, and his heart broke as each morning he saw the dead bodies that had been tossed on the curb. There were so many dying each day that the morgue couldn't handle it. Tens of thousands lived in this eleven-story ghetto area in Kowloon. They lived in small rooms (or shelves) stacked on top of each other. On the top, many lived in tents of cloth or cardboard and threw their sewage and trash over the sides. The bottom stories had no natural light. Many were drug addicts, and there was much drug-related crime. There was no sewage system, and the water supply was only a few pipes supplied by the Hong Kong Government.

It touched Rev. Chan's heart, and he began this outreach to Chinese drug addicts. Some of the recovering addicts have become leaders and are directing drug rehab centers in other areas of Southeast Asia. The Hong Kong Government ranks this as the most successful drug rehab and provided the use of Dawn Island for one dollar a year.

Dawn Island was surrounded by the sea, so the only way recovering drug addicts could get off the island was to swim. There were two shipping containers that were converted to bedrooms where newly arrived addicts were prayed through withdrawals. Once through the withdrawals, they joined the other overcomers on the island to learn living skills and the Word of God. They attended Bible studies learning about Jesus as Savior and Lord of their new lives.

Five English-speaking addicts had arrived from Nagaland, and they did not speak Chinese. Rev. Chan was looking for someone who would teach an English Bible study out on the island. That's where David entered the picture. He was asked to take a day a week and meet with the Naga guys. His first reaction was, "Where is Nagaland?" He soon learned it was located in the northeast corner of India. The inhabitants were tribal versus Indian. At the end of the nineteenth century, a missionary went to Nagaland, and many came to Christ. In fact, shortly after the turn of the century, the majority were Christians. As years passed, liberalism crept in and many became nominal Christians. Additionally, the drug lords operating in the Golden Triangle began giving young Naga guys cough syrup to hook them, and then they craved harder drugs. The drug lords would go to the parents and solicit money. If the parents refused, the young men were soon killed.

David accepted the challenge and was blessed. He met with the Nagas in a small concrete building with wooden shutters where the South China Sea surf sloshed up to the doorway (minus any actual door). The window openings let in light (minus any glass or screens). They sat around two desks pushed together and spent about three hours studying the Bible. Noontime came and homemade noodles were piled into a bowl along with a chicken wing, and everyone thought they were having a great feast. Each trip to Dawn Island, David would take along meat, a cake, or a bag of oranges. The only electricity on the island was produced by a gasoline generator. There was a tape player, so David gave the Naga guys audiotapes of preaching and Gospel music. These guys were so hungry for the Word of God and wanted to share it. They asked David for copies of the lessons so they could send them to their families in Nagaland.

To get to Dawn Island was no small task. First, David had to take a taxi to the train, then change to a double-decker bus, and at the end of the line take a minibus, finally reaching the small port about an hour later. Now to get to the island, it took another hour on a junk. Some had a small shelter on board, and people actually lived on them. One week, the trip was frightening because the old Chinese lady who sat at the junk wheel apparently couldn't see very well and headed into the path of a large fishing boat. The Chinese captain of that boat yelled something in Chinese, and she was able to swerve and miss it.

David had been invited to speak on Father's Day to both the Chinese and English speakers, and I was invited to go along. As we dressed, we noticed it was a stormy day. We were all set to go, and we went down the three flights of stairs to hail a taxi. We stepped out in the street and the monsoon rains were coming at us sideways. We were drenched immediately. Usually there was a junk in the harbor to take us to Dawn Island, but today our friends had sent a small, open motorboat to fetch us. Picture this—in the small boat, driver at the rear manning the motor, and the two of us with umbrellas raised to protect from the rain. We maneuvered around the boats in the harbor and through a maze of islands. The Naga guys were already on the dock when we arrived to help us out of the boat. The rain had stopped, but coming down over the stairs that we needed to climb was a waterfall. David and I rolled up our pant legs, and holding on to one of the Naga guys, we forged the falls. At the top of the hill were dilapidated concrete buildings with metal roofs. Yes, the day was filled with showers of blessings!

More blessings came in a few days with a phone call from friends in Atlanta. Michael and Michelle wanted to know how we were and what we needed. Michael talked with David about what God was doing in our lives. Then Michael said, "The Lord brought you to my mind, and we have decided to send a check to your ministry for your support. We are going to send five thousand dollars." David started crying, overwhelmed with such a blessing. They continued to be a blessing to us. When we left Hong Kong, months later the investment counsel Michael had given had earned thirty-two percent.

I was asked to teach a Sunday school class of Filipino ladies. Traveling around Hong Kong I had seen lots of Filipino ladies. Sometimes on Sunday afternoons there would be hundreds of them in central Hong Kong. I was told that here in Hong Kong, most Chinese are workaholics. Making money seems to be at the center of their lives, and they work long hours, and the family unit suffers. Most Hong Kong families (except the poor ones) have an amah that is a maid and nanny. Hundreds of Filipinos come to Hong Kong to work as amahs and send money home to their families. They usually live with the family in a small room about the size of a closet. They do the housework, cooking and caring for the children. Many children know the amah as their mother, since she gets them up in the morning, and before their parents come home, they are in bed. I fell in love with these sweet, hardworking ladies. I heard their stories about not being able to find work in the Philippines and sacrificing by coming to Hong Kong in order to help feed their children at home.

I had the privilege of teaching the book *Lifetime Guarantee* by Bill Gillham. It is one of my favorite books about not living our life for Christ, but trusting Christ to express His life through us, by faith. Teaching these ladies took me back to the days when I was crying out for help. And like these ladies, I was still learning to trust each day.

"Blessed be the God and Father of our Lord Jesus Christ, the Father of mercies and God of all comfort, who comforts us in all our affliction, so that we may be able to comfort those who are in any affliction, with the comfort with which we ourselves are comforted by God" (2 Cor. 1:3–4).

One Sunday, Phil Yang showed up in my class, and it just happened to be the day we had invited the class to come to our apartment for a fellowship lunch after church. After class, he accepted an invitation to come too. Phil was twenty-five years old and was a Chinese born in New York City. His parents were from Hong Kong, and he had recently come to Hong Kong to establish a trading business. During class, he told that he was not a believer but was interested in learning about Christianity.

We had lunch at our apartment, and the ladies began to leave. Phil lingered on until everyone was gone. David was busy answering Phil's questions about the Bible and Jesus. Toward evening, Phil said he wanted to accept Jesus and become a Christian. David led him through the sinner's prayer. After he asked Jesus into his heart to be his Savior and Lord, he said that a long time ago he had selected another name but never had used it. He pulled out a business card already printed with his other name, "Christian Yang." Incredible! He came in Phil and went out Christian. From then on, he introduced himself as Christian Yang. Christian continued to come by and study the Bible with David.

There were times of refreshment when Stuart and Jill Briscoe came to Hong Kong for a week of Bible teaching at Keswick Convention. I had heard Jill speak years ago at The Peoples Church in Toronto. David was asked to speak to the Filipino group at Central-City Hall, and on Mother's Day I spoke to the Filipino Fellowship on Forgiving Our Mothers. We also had visits from special friends like Chuck, his Chinese wife, and his son, who was now a toddler. They came to stay with us a couple of days on their way to Saudi Arabia to teach English. Another friend, Edie, who worked with us in Friends from Abroad came to visit. Edie and her husband had gone to China several years ago. She was pregnant and coming from China to Hong Kong to have her baby. We were thrilled to see her and have her stay with us when she came for her prenatal checkups. When delivery time came, we went to see the new baby at the hospital up on the Peak on Hong Kong Island.

During our time in Hong Kong, we tried to learn Mandarin. We had a tutor, but neither David nor I had any musical ability or an ear for the different tones. It may have been some of our most humorous times when we tried to get those many tones to come out of our mouths. I will always remember David doing the rising tone as he lifted his chin resting on his chest to pointing it toward the ceiling to express it. Living in the middle of a Cantonese-speaking culture made it more difficult. I had heard you better get the tone right or it might be embarrassing when you say "may": it could mean "you are beautiful" or "you are a horse."

The last three months in Hong Kong, we did research on China for a mission agency. They wanted help developing a training manual to assist American business people going into China. We had the privilege to lead the study: 'Experiencing God' at Lionel and Karen's. They were friends who lived at Discovery Bay on Lantau Island just off Hong Kong. It took about an hour and a half to get there via bus and boat. We met Lionel and Karen at church, and they were Canadians from Vancouver working in Hong Kong as principal and vice principal at an international school. They provided a great deal of support and fellowship. During our ups and downs and near-drowning experiences, we need each other for encouragement. God has put so many people in my path to do just that.

"And let us consider how to stir up one another to love and good works, not neglecting to meet together, as is the habit of some, but encouraging one another, and all the more as you see the Day drawing near" (Heb. 10:24–25).

GOD AND GOD ALONE

Our lives have been so rich since we said yes to the Lord and left the corporate world. I could continue to fill many, many pages with the blessings the Lord has given over the years. We had to sacrifice not being with family and friends, and our family and friends sacrificed too.

In Luke 12, Jesus tells us not to be anxious about our life, what we will eat, nor about our body, nor what we will put on. He provides for the raven and we are more valuable. He clothes the lilies even finer than Solomon in all his glory. He continues saying that the nations of the world seek after these things, and our Father knows we all need them. But then He says, "Instead, seek His kingdom and these things will be added to you" and "For where your treasure is, there will your heart be also."

Our Chinese friend, Mary, wrote, "I think I'm closer to God than at any time in my life." She had been reading the Bible we gave her. I learned a couple of years later that she had married an American and moved to the State of Virginia. She said her mother-in-law was a Christian, and she had become a Christian.

There were those special moments with the Naga guys. A few years later, one of them became a missionary to tribal people in another part of Southeast Asia.

When I hear anyone singing "It is Well with My Soul," I think of walking arm-in-arm with Gloria through the streets of Macau. God transformed the casino dealer to a child of God. I wonder what happened to Christian Yang. Did he expand his trading business in China and share his new life in Christ?

There was the young lady in the guesthouse who asked what Christmas was all about, and the man on the mountain who was so happy when he got a copy of the Bible. And I think about Nara, who I met when she was sitting next to the path in Toronto, and Auntie and family in Macau. I pray that I will see them in heaven. Praise the Lord for opportunities that He provided for us to share His Word with them.

I heard Ravi Zacharias on the radio recently saying that the church in China is the fastest growing church in the world. There are estimates that there will be 247 million Christians living in China by 2030. That will be higher than the US, which currently holds the title of largest Christian population.

I read that one professor in China told a Christian colleague to stop criticizing Marxism because it left the souls of the people empty, and that is why they were listening now. I can just hear a generation from now someone telling the next generation of preachers in America, "Stop criticizing naturalism. It has left the souls of people empty, which is why they are listening to you now."

It seems like many Christians are up in arms these days about political issues, Supreme Court decisions and how the new culture is ruining America. Perhaps we should spend more time on our knees asking the Lord to continue to bring people to the end of themselves where they will be receptive to His saving grace. Perhaps we should get out of the comfortable "holy huddle" and let our light shine brightly in the darkness of our world.

I can still remember that Sunday morning when Dr. Charles Stanley said, "We don't pray big enough." He challenged the congregation to ask God for something big, and then we paused to pray. Later, David and I compared our prayers and we had both prayed for China to become a Christian nation. May the Lord continue to answer that prayer!

I think of Edie, who has been in China with her family as missionaries for over twenty five years now. I wonder what impact their lives have had on bringing China closer to becoming a Christian nation.

The most important thing I learned through these years was "God and God alone." To trust the Lord when I cannot figure out the reason for why it is happening, to trust Him when it appears to be an inconvenience, to trust God when I don't see an answer and the bottom line, to trust Him at all times.

When we left Hong Kong for the second time, we called time out and wandered through nine European countries over an eleven-week period. We each had a rolling suitcase and a small carry on. We planned our trip to stay in mission guesthouses with a whole week at Capernwray, one of Ian Thomas's Torchbearer Bible Schools. Capernwray Hall is a nineteenth century castle just south of England's famous Lake District. When we got back to the USA, the investment Michael had recommended had made enough money during those eleven weeks to pay for the entire trip.

David and I continued on the "spirit-led life" and it was usually not a "logic-led life." We said yes to four more mission assignments, mostly around the Mediterranean. In February 2001, we settled down and stopped moving in and out of the USA. David went to be with the Lord in 2014, and I began to learn about living "Life after David". Another chapter in my life.

God is with us during the hard times and the good times, encouraging and sustaining us through this journey called life. "He put a new song in my mouth, a song of praise to our God. Many will see and fear and put their trust in the LORD" (Ps.40:3). "Therefore, we are ambassadors for Christ, God making His appeal through us. We implore you on behalf of Christ, be reconciled to God" (2 Cor. 5:20).

AUTHOR'S END NOTE

I told you in the Introduction how Jesus was always there, taking me by the hand and teaching me more about God and God alone.

Peter instantly obeyed God. Do you know Jesus as your Savior and Lord? Are you willing to follow Him?

Peter witnessed Jesus providing everything he needed. Do you trust Jesus to provide?

God is in control, and He knew the disciples were headed for problems. It was no surprise to Him. Are you willing to let Him handle your problems?

Peter was frightened and had that sinking feeling. Will you give your fears to God?

God says, "Trust me." Will you let Him direct your life?

Consider the following scriptures and make the most important decision you will ever make.

Romans 3:23, *"For all have sinned, and fall short of the glory of God."*

We have all sinned. We have all done things that are displeasing to God.

Romans 6:23, *"For the wages of sin is death, but the free gift of God is eternal life through Jesus Christ our Lord."*

The punishment that we have earned for our sins is death. Not just physical death, but eternal death! God's solution to our sin is a gift that can't be earned.

Romans 5:8, *"But God shows His own love for us, in that while we were still sinners, Christ died for us."*

Jesus Christ died for us! Jesus' death paid for the price of our sins. Jesus' resurrection proves that God accepted Jesus' death as the payment for our sins.

Romans 10:9, *"If you confess with your mouth that Jesus is Lord, and believe in your heart that God raised Him from the dead, you will be saved."*

Because of Jesus' death on our behalf, all we have to do is believe in Him, trusting His death as the payment for our sins, and we will be saved!

Romans 10:13, *"For everyone who calls on the name of the Lord will be saved."*

Jesus died to pay the penalty for our sins and rescue us from eternal death. Salvation, the forgiveness of sins, is available to anyone who will trust in Jesus Christ as their Lord and Savior.

Romans 5:1, *"Therefore, since we have been justified through faith, we have peace with God through our Lord Jesus Christ."*

Through Jesus Christ, we can have a relationship of peace with God.

Romans 8:1, *"Therefore, there is now no condemnation for those who are in Christ Jesus."*

Romans 8:38-39, *"For I am sure that neither death nor life, nor angels nor rulers, nor things present nor things to come, nor powers, nor height nor depth, nor anything else in all creation, will be able to separate us from the love of God in Christ Jesus our Lord."*

Would you like to receive Christ as your Savior? If so, here is a simple prayer you can pray to God. Saying this prayer is a way to declare to God that you are relying on Jesus Christ for your salvation. The words themselves will not save you. Only faith in Jesus Christ can provide salvation and new life!

"God, I know that I have sinned against you and am deserving of punishment. But Jesus Christ took the punishment that I deserve so that through faith in Him I could be forgiven. With your help, I place my trust in you for salvation. Thank you for your wonderful grace and forgiveness and the gift of eternal life! I ask that you direct my life from now on. Amen!"

SUGGESTED READING

George, Bob. *Classic Christianity,* Harvest House Publishers, 1989.

Gillham, Bill. *Lifetime Guarantee,* Eugene, OR, Harvest House, 1993.

LeFebre, Lee. *The Shackling of Grace,* Lee LeFebre Castle Pines, CO, 2013.

Nee, Watchman. *The Normal Christian Life,* Fort Washington, PA. Christian Literature Crusade,1979.

Solomon, Charles. *Handbook to Happiness,* Tyndale House, 1989, 1999.

Solomon, Charles. *The Ins and Out of Rejection,* Solomon Publications, 1991.

REFERENCES

1   Mueller, George. "George Mueller Quotes" http://christian-quotes.ochristian.com/George-Mueller-Quotes/ (accessed on May 2, 2017).

2   Mueller, George. "George Meuller Quotes" http://christian-quotes.ochristian.com/George-Mueller-Quotes/ (accessed on May 2, 2017).

3   Kaillo, Craig, M. "Gospel Interruptions" http://www.ststephensor.com/serarchiv/ser060730.htm/ (accessed January 22, 2017).

4   Carmichael, Amy. "Quotes from Amy Carmichael" http://www.liveatthewell.org/quotes-from-amy-carmichael.html/ (accessed February 2, 2017).

CPSIA information can be obtained
at www.ICGtesting.com
Printed in the USA
LVOW11s1957270917
550330LV00001B/19/P